Florence R

RE-FIRING
Not
RETIRING

EDITED BY
David Falkus MCIJ

Spirit of Caleb
Ministries

GUILDFORD • SURREY

RE-FIRING *Not* RETIRING
(the book)

First published in 2007 by
SPIRIT OF CALEB MINISTRIES *
2 Great Quarry,
Guildford, Surrey, GU1 3XN, United Kingdom

ISBN 978-1-906317-00-3

Initial contact with the publisher, David Falkus
(**member:** Chartered Institute of Journalists – freelance division;
The Christian Broadcasting Council;
The Full Gospel Business Men's Fellowship International
and the Parable Trust)

via *david@inspiredmedia.biz*
website: *www.inspiredmedia.biz*

* **Spirit of Caleb Ministries** is a **business ministry** whose object is to
further the Kingdom of God by spreading the Gospel of Jesus Christ

Produced and printed by members of
THE GUILD OF MASTER CRAFTSMEN

Cover Design by Cecil Smith and David Falkus
Book Design and Typesetting by Cecil Smith
Typeset in Giovanni Book

Printed and bound in Great Britain by
RPM PRINT & DESIGN
2-3 Spur Road, Quarry Lane, Chichester, West Sussex PO19 8PR

Contents

Introduction to

VideoBook Publishing by Spirit of Caleb Ministries

Ever since Gutenberg invented printing from moveable type and Caxton set up his press in England, there have been an ever-increasing flood of books. For the last few years there has been an ever-increasing flood of DVDs. DVDs mostly came in expensive cases. So there were books (even books with CDs) – and then there were DVDs – two different entities.

But it struck me just a few weeks ago that there could be 'VideoBooks' – where 'readers' would not merely inspired by vivid words leaping off the printed page – wonderful as that taken-for-granted miracle can be – but there inside the back cover would be a full-length DVD enabling you – in your home, perhaps in a home group or larger setting – to virtually "meet the author". Ideally the in-depth studio interview would be interspersed with video clips of the author in action, say on a Mercy Ship or in Africa! Once you've watched the DVD; you can **read the printed book with these images in your mind**.

According to tradition, an apple falling off a tree inspired Sir Isaac Newton to start pondering on the mysteries of gravity. The 'apple' that fell off my 'tree' was Florence Robertson! In July 2004 she phoned me; we met. After a week of frantic research to get her story and – crucially helped by her daughters in the USA – her video material lined up, I did the 56-minute "live" TV studio interview with her. Failing to find for her an existing publisher willing to do more than publish some of Florence's exploits, **Spirit of Caleb Ministries** publishers of **VideoBooks** has been birthed in 2007 – I can finally publish her book – and inside the back cover is the DVD of that 2004 *Spirit of Caleb* interview.

David Falkus

Publisher's
Acknowledgements

I am very grateful to Howard and Lesley Conder, founders of *Revelation TV*, for responding to my October 2003 letter suggesting *Spirit of Caleb* programming, and inviting me to come the following year into the television studio which they were having constructed, bringing in guests – mature Christians of great faith in a great God – for a lunchtime 56-minute interview once a week, for 12 weeks. The *Spirit of Caleb* TV series began on June 2nd 2004 with David Hathaway, Founder and President of Eurovision.

My thanks also to the Conders for agreeing that, since they could not pay me for months of work, I would hold the residual rights; to my guests for coming into the studio and also agreeing to further use of the 12 recordings. *The disciples being told to gather the remains of a miraculous feast in 12 baskets* came to mind, and the 12 *Spirit of Caleb* programmes later ran and re-ran for several months in 2006 on Premier TV – and there are many other channels out there!)

Many thanks, too, to the *Revelation TV* crew, mostly volunteers, who worked tirelessly behind the scenes in 2004; to Phil Maltz who created the opening and closing graphics just the evening before the first show, and especially to my good friend Steve Jefferies, handling guests' video material, skilfully directing the shows – ten of which went out "live to air" over the SKY satellite, and periodically giving a mix of time-cues and encouraging words into the tiny earpiece in my right ear.

Amongst many friends who have encouraged me over the years, I would especially like to thank journalist Tony Russell who in 1989 encouraged me to join the Chartered Institute of Journalists – thus opening up a whole new world of opportunity to me; my then pastor Revd Bob Roxburgh for arranging in 1984 the help which got a virtually unemployed me on my first-of-seven visits to the USA in 1985; the couple in my church who prayed over my badly-injured right knee so that I got on the pre-booked flight to the USA with only one stick and not two; Les Raker (met in the UK through the Revd Robin

Rees and then owning a Christian TV station in Manassas VA) for inviting me over to 'observe' – and, during that visit, the preacher in Woodbridge VA who, with no clue from me but given a 'word of knowledge', said *"Right knee – in Jesus' Name – Be healed!"*

I flew back – with no stick – also remembering a Gospel Outreach house-group who gathered round and prophesied over me, and their pastor Joe Esposito who turned to me on the Sunday and said: "David, the Lord has given me a 'word' for you regarding the work He wants you to do. *"Do not take on too many things. At first you will have to do many things – but after that you will narrow down your work."* – a 'word' which I believe is now – after 22 years of "doing many things" – reaching its fulfilment.

I am also very grateful to Florence's daughters Lynn, Francine and her husband David O'Connor, CFRE, Foundations Manager, Mercy Ships, for supplying between them the photographs for the 4-page colour section and the DVD graphics; also to Diane Rickard, Mercy Ships UK, for providing the photograph of the *Anastasis* for the front cover.

Very grateful to many other long-time friends, especially the long-time friend whose generosity made this very recent **VideoBook** dream a reality, I must especially thank my prophetically-gifted friend Andrew Baker of Makeway Ministries firstly for the 'word' in 1992 that I and another Christian TV pioneer were "to have the Spirit of Caleb."

Then, a few weeks before the 2004 *Spirit of Caleb* TV series, I phoned Andrew in Spain and asked him to seek the Lord for a 'word' about it. A night or two later, the Lord woke him up and gave him a full prophetic teaching on "What the Spirit of Caleb IS". Andrew wrote it out for me. (see page 107).

Florence has the *Spirit of Caleb*, in the fullest measure. So it is wonderfully fitting that her book – the **book** the Lord promised her when she was in Canada more than a decade ago – is the key part of my first **VideoBook** publication. In affectionately honouring her, I am reminded of the verse (I Sam 2.30) handed – in the film, as had happened decades before in real life – to the hero of *Chariots of Fire*:

"Those that honour Me – I will honour..."

David Falkus

Author's Acknowledgements

I would like to thank those who invited me to join them on outreaches, particularly Youth With A Mission, and Mercy Ships for inviting me to come onboard and evangelise on 14 occasions. I would also like to thank those whose encouragement and practical/financial support assisted me in going.

Grateful acknowledgment is made to David Falkus for his help, hard work, and constant encouragement in getting out this book; to Master Craftsman Cecil Smith for his very skilful book design and book creation work, to Jonathan Harry, the Managing Director of RPM Print & Design Ltd, Chichester, and the rest of his staff who printed the book, bound it and inserted the DVDs inside the back cover – just in time for my 87th birthday... and to Don Stephens, Founder/President of Mercy Ships, busy with the arival in Liberia of the *African Mercy*, for sending me a personal message. I also very much appreciate the forewords by Lynn and Marti Green, Co-Founders of YWAM UK.

On the DVD side, I would like to thank David Boyden of TwobyTwoWorship Ltd, Chesterfield, who spent many hours fine-tuning the digital material of my 2004 TV interview. He and his wife Julie then produced hundreds of beautifully-printed DVDs.

***Finally, thanks be to God for His grace
in using me and taking me on
such a wonderful and exciting journey.***

Florence Robertson

Forewords

from Lynn and Marti Green
YWAM, Youth With A Mission UK

LYNN GREEN wrote:

Every person is unique, but some people are more than unique – they are memorable characters! Florence Robertson is one of those. If you have met Florence, you will remember her.

When I first met Florence, she was working for an airline at London's Gatwick airport. But I recognised two character qualities which Florence expressed in an unusual manner. Most obvious was the fact that she loved Jesus intensely; her gratitude to Him for her salvation came bubbling out of her. Secondly, I was forcibly struck by her boldness. This was no carefully-balanced, reserved English woman; this was a firebrand! And she was burning to be more radical and significant for Jesus.

Shortly after that first meeting, Florence took early 'retirement' and embarked on an amazing series of adventures in the Kingdom of God. Throughout the years that followed, she demonstrated an unflinching commitment to do whatever God wanted her to do. That kind of radical obedience will always lead to God's radical provision of all our needs.

You might be tempted to doubt the accuracy of the stories which follow because they are so remarkable. I would be surprised if you were tempted to think that they are somewhat exaggerated. But I can vouch for Florence's honesty and the accuracy of her memory!

Many would also be tempted to think. "That's okay for Florence Robertson, but I am not like that." But this book is primarily about God and He is always the same – for everyone.

It seems to me that each person has a huge potential for growth, to become much more than we are, spiritually, emotionally and mentally. However, few of us grow to that great potential. Some do. Why? Because they have learnt to step out of their 'comfort zones.'

When she was already in her sixties, Florence Robertson stepped well beyond her comfort zone into a series of obedient adventures where, without God's help, she would not have survived. As a result, she has grown in wisdom, knowledge, love and experience for a further 20 years and more.

Few readers of this book will have the same personality as Florence, but each of us can seek to imitate her love for God and her boldness on His behalf. If we do, the God of Florence Robertson's adventures will be the God of our adventures.

In His Peace,
Lynn Green

(International Chairman, Youth With A Mission),

MARTI GREEN wrote:

Florence Robertson is one of the most selfless women I have had the privilege of knowing. Her burning passion and faithfulness to share Jesus' love and power has been the hallmark of her life. When many would have settled back and retired into their later years, Florence's first-hand knowledge of the forgiveness of her Lord, and gratitude for all He had done in her life, urged her to shores others only read and dream about. The pages of her stories that follow will challenge you to get up and go to wherever God calls you, to step out into the adventure and joy that await you in the hidden corners of this globe.

Florence has always given full glory to God for His power at work through her as she simply dared to believe He could do miracles. She has never been afraid to be out on a limb, in a place where she knew that, if God didn't come through, there was no way back.

She has been no respecter of persons and valued none above another. If age and physical frailty had not caught up with her, today she would still be out in some village in Africa or Asia, sharing her five loaves and two fishes.

Florence has known what it means when Paul said, *"For me to live is Christ..."* May you know this truth in greater revelation as you read these pages and then follow Him who opened the gates of heaven for you and me.

Marti Green

Co-founder (with husband Lynn)
of Youth With A Mission England

87th Birthday Message
from Don Stephens,
Founder/President, Mercy Ships

Deyon and I have known Florence since her teen-aged daughter Francine, now O'Connor, left her job with British European Airways to serve with Mercy Ships. Francine was amongst the earliest crew to live and serve on the first ship *Anastasis* while in Venice, Italy. Since that time, we came to know her sister Lynn, and Florence.

Florence actually joined her daughter Francine and served onboard the *Anastasis* for periods of time. Her unique personality, prayers and perseverance are remembered by one and all.

Florence, just a few moments ago, we finished the 'last community meeting' onboard the ship that was the launching of this organization. While we all rejoiced in the arrival of our new hospital ship *Africa Mercy*, we are also celebrating a series of 'last time to do this'. We have planned our 'last community meeting', our last meal – that some called 'the last supper' with no dis-respect to our Saviour, and many other lasts. I specifically mentioned the 'many that were not present' who prayed, gave and served onboard. You are one of these faithful servants.

I also mentioned a few of those who have gone on before us, Alan Williams [UK and New Zealand], Annette Geike [USA], and Ofa Tanioa [Tonga]. Each was a vital part of Mercy Ships and is now a part of the great cloud of witnesses of whom the author of Hebrews 11 writes so movingly. Somehow, I sensed they were watching us tonight.

God bless you on this your 87th birthday!

With love and respect to you and your extended family.

Don

An Appreciation
from her two daughters and her son

As we contemplate the legacy our mother leaves in the nations where she shared the gospel, we cannot help but find the connection between her life and many of the heroes memorialized in the Scriptures. She has a boldness and tenacity that few can equal. Within the focus of her numerous ministry trips, her willingness to step out in faith made an impact not only on those with whom she shared the Gospel but also on her co-labourers in the Kingdom. We continue to be amazed at how many people her indomitable spirit has left a mark on.

Joshua 24 inspires us with the words,

"As for me and my house, we will serve the Lord."

Our mother chose to overlook her faults and shortcomings, and devote her latter years to dedication to the cause of Christ. No matter an individual's economic status, nationality, social position, or age, her deep compassion for the broken people of our world was evident to all those with whom she came in contact.

Florence's legacy to us is far from traditional but one that is lasting. Her example speaks of a willingness to expect great things from God, to step out in faith, fully anticipating an answer and a way forward. Her testimony is one of great redemption, of God taking what was broken and moulding it into a vessel worthy of His service.

In many cultures, her 'grey head' gave her an instant platform and position of respect. Even in this position of esteem, she would not hesitate to set aside pride and decorum to hold a child or an adult on her lap and speak words of comfort and strength. The floor of a mud hut in Africa was where she slept. The table of an impoverished labourer was where she ate. Alongside the evangelist, the healthcare worker, the aid worker is where she conveyed the heart of her saviour.

With blue eyes sparkling and a voice of authority and determination, she refused to let her age slow her down even into her '80s. Even now while the flesh is weakening, the spirit refuses to let go of her Anchor in life, as she takes comfort in the scriptures and in the words of her Father and her Redeemer.

Our reflection on her legacy leaves a feeling of great hope as we embrace a life that made a radical change of course mid-stream and cast aside every encumbrance to run the race that was set before her with perseverance. Truly, we are surrounded by a great cloud of witnesses, who will one day join those who remain in the land of the living to hear our Lord say,

"Well done, my good and faithful servant."

With our love,

Lynn (Robertson) Stiles
Francine (Robertson) O'Connor
Ian Robertson

The Author's
introduction to herself – and
her not-retiring adventures begin

*"Go into all the world
preaching the gospel."*
Matt. 28 (18-20)

The bombs were falling as we huddled in our air raid shelter. It was September, 1940. My father was in bed in our home, too sick to be moved. He was 51 years old. I was 20. At dawn I learned that a bomb had hit our house, my father had been thrown out of bed and had died. A new phase of my life begun.

Eventually the war ended with many of my friends gone forever. All I wanted was to escape, so I wrote to my uncle in Australia and expressed my ardent desire to go there. He, being influential, sent a ticket and £100. I sailed on 1st January 1947 for thirty-one unbroken days at sea via South Africa to Freemantle, Western Australia. Another phase of my life began. Sadly, I had a chip on my shoulder. Had I not lost the best years of my life? Didn't somebody owe me something? I came to take, not to give to Australia.

My uncle was Manager of Ford Company for Queensland. He met me in Sydney and we drove up the Gold Coast (1,000 miles plus) to Brisbane. I secured a singing spot with ABC (Australian Broadcasting Commission) but first we went driving into arid desert to visit Ford dealers.

Wow! Suddenly I had to have an emergency tonsillectomy. Since then I've been singing with the tenors! So, with no singing career, it was back to work with Shell Company. The difference between a job in London and Brisbane was that in Brisbane every Friday you said, "Who's for the Beach?" Someone was always going. So, you took off for the weekend to Surfers Paradise which **was** paradise in those days with thirty-three miles of white sand and hardly any people. There I became a weekend lady lifeguard.

This all sounds idyllic – it wasn't. Life with uncle was volcanic, to say the least, so I returned to Britain via the Suez Canal, Egypt and Malta in August 1948. The next phase had begun. That autumn I became a Butlin's Redcoat in Ayr, Scotland. One of my functions was to fall, fully clothed from the 3-metre diving board pretending to be a spectator trying to get a better view of the gala. The handsome high diver was supposed to rescue me. The campers loved that, but I didn't, as the water never got above 50 degrees Fahrenheit and I nearly froze while he combed his hair! However I did get to escort senior campers to the Electric Brae, Robbie Burns Cottage and other sights.

One season being enough, I returned to London. That's where I met my husband. We were married in July 1950, then left for a honeymoon in Europe. Just in case this sounds normal, it wasn't. We hiked across France arriving in Geneva without funds and were sent to a Swiss Farm to work on the Grape Harvest. We were privileged to sleep in the barn with horses and rats rather than with the seasonal regulars from France (Savoyards)! Suspicious of us at first, our hosts became our good friends. They had never had a 'Brit' doing the work before. It is very hard work, by the way.

Harvest over, my husband took another farm job, while I walked in a dress and with high heeled shoes, from our cheap accommodation in Annemasse, France, to Geneva in Switzerland. First I, then my husband, found employment with international organisations… and so eighteen years passed.

In August 1968 and with three children, we had financial problems, so I applied for a job with IATA (International Air Transport Association). I was the only applicant so was given the job despite not having worked a comptometer for 18 years. One of the perks was cheap or even free travel, with most airlines. That's when my life hit the rapids. My husband went to a Conference and did not return to us.

We had recently moved and were surrounded by Christians who were praying for this dysfunctional family. In 1969 my children became Christians through neighbours, Christian teachers and Campus Crusade. When they told me I said, "So am I". My younger daughter said, "No, mummy, you are not. You drink, smoke, swear and speak about others. You also fought with daddy." I was shocked, but it still took another year before on October 15th 1970, I gave my life to Jesus. I was 50 and had sat in churches nearly all my life – even sung in a choir for three years – so I was angry that all that long time I had thought that

I was a Christian but wasn't – and I told the Lord that I would preach the gospel and challenge as many people as I could before I died.

That's when Satan tried to kill me. I had to work every Christmas and New Year. Whilst working on December 31st 1970 when all Swiss celebrate St. Sylvestre, I suffered a ruptured duodenal ulcer. It seems I would have died but for the Swiss Army who were on duty at the airport because it was the era of hijackers. An army doctor diagnosed and sent me to hospital by army truck. No doctors being available on that day, someone sent for the Chief Medical Officer who performed an emergency operation. My Christian neighbour looked after my 12 and 10-year old children that New Year's Eve. My eldest was in Scotland training to be a nurse and that's when I knew God had a purpose for our lives.

In October '73 the Lord said "This is not your land, return to Britain". I wept. Christians prayed and all agreed that I would get much more help in NHS Britain! I said "Yes" and that's when the Lord parted the Red Sea for us. I sold or gave away possessions. Air India gave us free travel to London. I had a job lined up with British Caledonian Airline in Crawley. Someone gave me a car that brought my husband home, with a few precious possessions. We had eight cardboard boxes with us.

Whilst packing I needed another emergency operation for a hernia which delayed us, so it was January 19th 1974 before we arrived in Britain. My husband elected again not to join us. A pastor had found me furnished accommodation in a large house which the owner had been trying to empty of guests in order to sell for two years. The rent was £5 per week when the going rate was £20-plus for one room! We had the use of three apartments!

It was the time of the merging of BOAC and BEA and they were making hundreds of staff redundant. So I thanked God for a job with British Caledonian in Crawley.

Ten months later BCAL had problems. Fellow workers assured me that "last in, first out" meant me. My landlady said, "House sold, you will have to go by Christmas." The headmaster said, "Your children should be attending the nearest school to where you live. They must change at Christmas." The church we were attending was too far to walk and we no longer had a car. I cried out to God "HELP!"

At 10am the next morning the Council housing manager phoned

me saying "I have a house for you to see. Can you collect the key and go and see it in your lunch hour?" I was so amazed I didn't even ask where or why. The manager said I had this offer because I was on BCAL's "key worker" list for priority housing, so that meant I wasn't going to lose my job. The house turned out to be halfway between our church and the school my children were attending. God answered all four issues the very next morning! I still live in this house, which is a constant reminder of our wonderful God who is pleased to answer our prayers and our cries for help. (My husband did come back, and spent many many years assisting me with my outreaches, until illness took him from me.)

In 1976 my daughter Francine took a YWAM "DTS" and "SOE"* and has worked in missions ever since. The next year my son took similar training, and I longed to go.

Retirement came in June 1980 when the pensions manager said, "Well Mrs Robertson you can draw some of your pension for a nice holiday or to decorate your house." I said, "What's the maximum I can take?" Reaching for a calculator he said, "£1,200, what are you going to do?" I said, "Go to school and then to missions." He was very surprised, commenting, " That's different."

I consulted Lynn Green (then director of YWAM England) as to where to go. Having retired from an airline, I had fare concessions with no geographical boundaries. He recommended the Crossroads Discipleship Training School (CDTS) for "Forties-Plus" in Kona, Hawaii, USA.

The next available CDTS was already fully booked up, so I had to wait until January 1981. Near the end, I discovered that there was to be no outreach, as we were "too old". I was devastated, so took time out to talk to the Lord. He told me to go to a cross-cultural School Of Evangelism on Oahu – that's another Hawaiian island.

Almost no-one had money. Many of the students were Islanders from Fiji, Samoa, and Hawaii. We had a Tongan leader. Even their churches couldn't support them.

* "DTS" **Discipleship Training School** and "SOE" **School of Evangelism** both run by Youth With A Mission (YWAM).

Loren Cunningham, the Founder-President of YWAM, came to speak to us. He said that the Lord had just changed his message to questions.

"Do you believe that God called you here?"

"Do you believe that the person next to you is also called?"

"Have you paid your fees?"

"Would you be prepared to give your outreach place to someone else?"

He added, "Seek the Lord for answers." Then he left.

We all did seek the Lord, of course, and I asked Him three more questions. I gave my neighbour my ticket down to Hong Kong. It was noon, so we went for lunch, during which the postman came. I received a cheque for US$750 from someone on my CDTS, so I took my ticket back and paid my neighbour's fees.

What, you may ask, were my three additional questions? The first was, "Is this You, Lord?" He gave me Genesis 28:15 – "I am with you and will keep you."

The second question was: "What about money?" He gave me Isaiah 55:1 – "Come, eat, drink without money."

Last, the big question: "What about my health?" He gave me Jeremiah 45:5, which began with "Do you seek great things for yourself? Seek them not!" I said, "Lord, I didn't ask You that." He said, "Read on!" So I did, and He said, "I will give you your life in all the places where you go." I have been running on these Scriptures ever since.

Despite having been a post-War lady lifesaver in Australia and a Butlin's Redcoat in Scotland, and having worked in Geneva for an international organisation for 25 years, those 23 years of "post-retirement mission" have been the most wonderful years of my life. I hope that as you read about them, they will give you inspiration to follow God wherever He takes you in this world and have similarly exciting years in your walk with Him.

Florence Robertson

Chapter 1

My first YWAM outreach: Singapore (June 1981)

Evangelism and "Going"! Those were the words that were to mark my first outreach experience, in 1981, as my School Of Evangelism (SOE) outreach team of 30 of us set out for our first destination – Hong Kong.

On arrival, we were given some further teaching from an organisation called Asian Outreach Hong Kong. This had been set up in 1966 by Paul Kauffman, when desperate refugees were streaming in from China and so many were responding to the gospel that the local churches were overwhelmed. So Paul wrote the *Living Word Bible Correspondence Course*, now being widely used in Asia, Africa and Latin America.

Mainly on evangelism and "going", the teaching was perfect for what was to come.

Our first efforts in evangelism were there in Hong Kong and the New Territories, and our first "going" involved smuggling Bibles into China – stories that I will leave until the next chapter. The next "going" brought the SOE team to Singapore, that island state off the southernmost tip of Malaysia, pulsating with life. More than 20 years later, I can still recall how spotlessly clean it was – an immediate fine would be imposed by police if litter of any kind, even a tiny piece of paper, was seen being dropped in the streets or public gardens.

The SOE team's first task in Singapore was to go out at night and make contact with the city-state's homosexuals, prostitutes and transvestites, each of which groups occupied a specific block in Orchard Street. I recall that the transvestites were incredibly beautiful and incredibly like women – it was just astounding that they were men. They were made up and had handbags and high heels and everything. It was almost unbelievable; I never saw anything like it in my life.

I felt deeply grieved in my spirit that they could not accept the gender that God had given them, and that they wanted to change it for another.

Many conversations took place, and some prayed to follow Jesus. I had strong feelings indeed when we sent a number of young men, whom we had talked to and who were interested in being discipled, to churches in the area – and the churches "just did not want to know". We know that Jesus would have received them.

After 20 days, we were split into teams of varying numbers, and then sent our separate ways to New Guinea, Java, Sabah, Brunei, Sarawak and Malaysia. I was in a team of five that spanned the generations (20-60 years old), mixed the colours (white, brown, yellow) and was led by a Texan and his Japanese-Hawaiian wife. We had to get to Ipoh, Malaysia, to staff a YWAM mini-DTS for one week and then go where the Spirit led: none of us had any funds. But God said to us, through my mouth, "As I fed the children of Israel for 40 years in the wilderness, is it too much for you to believe Me for seven weeks?" There was a shocked silence.

What is "outreach"?

To 'go on outreach' means that you are joining with other people to spread the gospel by any means. That can include teaching, preaching, praying, singing, witnessing by any and all means, that the gospel might be shed abroad.

A challenging story

While in Singapore, I had been attending the Baptist church in Changhi, and an English family had befriended me. One Sunday soon after the occasion when God spoke through me challenging our team to trust in His provision, this family had taken me to lunch at the father's club. To my shock, it was all drinking, smoking and rude jokes. The father was in the oil business.

That Sunday I asked him if he could give me a lift back to the YWAM centre, and he agreed. On the way, he was grumbling about the behaviour of his two sons, who were aged 17 and 13. He stopped at his home for something, and while I was waiting, his 13-year-old son walked in. I said, "A powerful man is speaking at the Methodist church in town tomorrow and I challenge you to go!" To my surprise, he quietly said, "I will", and disappeared into his room. Shortly after, the 17-year-old came in. I made the same challenge, and it received the same response. The father returned and we continued our journey.

Suddenly, I felt prompted to say, "You are the role model for your sons – and look at your lifestyle! The Bible says that Jesus will spew the lukewarm out of his mouth." At that, the man slammed on his brakes, opened the door on my side and screamed in rage, "Get out!" I did, and had to walk back to the centre in my high-heeled shoes. By the time I arrived, not only had I missed lunch, but everyone had gone off somewhere. I lay on my bed, disconsolately indulging in self-pity.

At 4pm, the guard said that there was someone to see me. It was the man's wife. She demanded, "Where is my husband?" I told her what had happened. She shouted, "Hallelujah! About time someone confronted him!" and drove off.

At 8pm, the guard again told me that there was someone to see me. This time it was the husband. He said, "Will you come to my house for dinner?" I politely declined, saying quite truthfully that I had already eaten. He persisted, so I finally accepted his invitation. The boys were there and heard their father, who ate nothing and smiled throughout the meal, say, "I've spent hours reviewing my life and repenting. Now I feel so clean. Please will you all forgive me?" Of course we did.

Later, the two boys told me that they had had a terrible fight when their parents were out and just before I came, and the 13-year-old boy had cried, "God! Send someone! We need help." The 17-year-old was all set to run away. Our God is omniscient and His timing is perfect.

When it was time to leave, the father put a roll of money into my hand and drove me back to the YWAM centre. The money, in several currencies, was enough to buy five single tickets to Pancor Island where, we had been told, a youth leader from Ipoh would come with funds and transport to take us the rest of the way to our destination.

Chapter 2

On to Pancor and Ipoh, Malaysia (1981)

We may only have stayed on Pancor Island for a few days, but our time there was full of supernatural events. First, we met a Swiss hippie who was so convicted of sin that he prayed for salvation, gave us his food and money, and left for his home. The next day I met two young men, one Chinese and the other Indian. They were playing Christian music. They said that their pastor was swimming. Our leader had already met him in the sea. That evening we worshipped the Lord together on the beach. They left the next day, leaving us food, utensils, and money, plus the promise of a string of churches where we could minister, be housed and fed, all the way back to Singapore. By the time our contact arrived three days later, we had funds to get to Ipoh and to pay for our stay on Pancor Island.

We arrived safely in Ipoh. There, we were housed in the home of a Buddhist, who owned a restaurant and sent us food every day. This was cooked by a darling tiny Chinese lady, about four foot-something tall, who stood over a wok which was heating at ground level. No-one could communicate with her, but we tried to convey our thanks, esteem and love.

Trials and tribulations

Being part of an SOE team on outreach was not without its trials. At one time, I shared a dormitory with 24 Chinese girls who were delightful but took no notice of repeated instructions to be quiet after 10pm, with lights-out at 10:30pm – so I didn't get much sleep. During our 'sharing' times, I had listened to all their problems and prayed for each one. Often, their fear was of Buddhist fathers who threatened that they would be thrown out onto the street if they became Christians.

Other night-time 'trials' from living in cramped quarters in one house came from two men, fellow members of our team – Larry (20), a Californian, and Hari (26) from Indonesia. Larry got up early in the morning and started strumming a guitar, and then he did press-ups at 6am. Hari played a guitar until the early hours of the morning. Put them together and there wasn't much chance of getting any sleep.

Then there were the cockroaches. One morning when I awoke, there were three dead ones under my body. Happily, I was completely covered as a result of the sleeping arrangements – under mosquito nets, fully dressed, on one of three mattresses on the floor, the other two being for Larry and Hari!

Our typical Malaysian shower was a small tiled room which had no pegs, nails, hooks etc. This was because, from a constantly-running tap, bricked in like a full-length sink, you throw water all over yourself using a plastic container or a small ceramic pot. I could not go in and out naked, so kept my clothes on and went, dripping wet, to our cramped toilet to change.

During this time, we ministered with and to the local youth until the early hours, sitting at hawker (outdoor food) stands, very different from their scrupulously clean counterparts in Singapore. We saw lots of rats, as women bathed babies in bowls alongside pans filled with boiling soup.

At the end of the week our leader from Singapore arrived with our post. I received a cheque for US$250 from a farming couple in Nebraska who had been with me on my Crossroads DTS. Relationships with the husband, who smoked and who categorically refused prayer on this issue, had not been easy. So this gift was totally unexpected, and healed my disappointment over my offer to pray for him being refused. My other team members, who would often receive funds in the post, on this occasion received nothing.

I knew from that first outreach the call of evangelist on my life. Preaching came naturally and I hungered to tell people – in ones or thousands – about Jesus. Also, after this outreach in Malaysia I had no difficulty in the subsequent 23 years in believing God to save, heal, deliver, provide, protect, and guide and to be confident that the weak are strong in Him.

The icing on the cake for me was that, on our return to Singapore, the family of four whom I had got to know there were waiting to greet me with flowers, gifts, and wonderful smiles. Both boys had responded and given their lives to Jesus at the Methodist meeting, and all the family had been baptised in the sea in my absence. One gift was a Bible with four photos of faces on the opening page with the scripture *Proverbs 8:6-10*. Glory to God!

Tales from Kuala Lumpur

Another example of God's perfect timing came when our team was in Kuala Lumpur. We had taken a large battery-operated tape-recorder and loudspeaker to a district of Kuala Lumpur that had a huge bus depot. There were people everywhere, the place was packed; every shop and café was blaring music. It was a ghastly cacophony of sound. We prayed against it and began to start our pathetic little show.

Suddenly, all electricity was cut: lights out, music silenced. We rapidly put on our tape, shouting to the crowds to come. When the first light came back on we immediately started singing. We rapidly got a large crowd around us before the rest of the lights came on. Before the police could locate us, we preached Jesus. One Malaysian woman was saved. The angels rejoiced.

The police not only moved us out, but on – everywhere that we tried to present Jesus. The next day they came to the house we were staying in, and escorted us out of the city centre to the outskirts. There a church rescued us, by bringing us to their building where they gave us food and shelter.

This led to the next wonderful story, one of many which resounds to the glory of God. We were back in Kuala Lumpur and attending a Sunday morning service at a Baptist church. The pastor said,

> **"Turn to the person on your right
> and ask them how they are, if you know them,
> and who they are, if you don't."**

I turned and had quite a shock as I saw a small, thin, dirty, smelly Chinese man dressed in rags. When I spoke to him, he smiled, revealing missing upper front teeth. He was not very old, perhaps in his 30s. He just had time before the service started to tell me that the police had suggested that he came to church to get help.

When the service finished, I turned to him and said, "Tell me about yourself."

He replied, "I have no home, so sleep on street; no job, so no money for clothes or food, so get whatever I can, sometimes from rubbish bin. Police keep moving me on." I asked him if he believed in Jesus? He nodded yes. At that, I cried out, asking the Lord to meet this poor man's need of home, job, food, clothes, and even dental treatment. The man smiled his thanks, and I left to rejoin my team.

After the service, it seemed that the whole church, together with our team, were invited to lunch at the beautiful home of a wealthy Chinese banker. We lined up and worked our way down the magnificent table spread with delectable and delicious dishes of every kind. Finding a seat, I enjoyed the feast. Replete, my eyes roved over many people present and those still lining up. To my amazement there he was, my poor Chinese man, wearing a smart pink striped shirt with cream trousers. Bursting with questions, I gave him time to enjoy his sumptuous meal before going over to him and asking, "What happened?"

He told me this story. "The man gave me a job as his gardener with a room of my own over the garage. He gave me new clothes, told me to take shower, and come get food. See Indian lady there, she dentist. Man spoke her, asked if she could help me. She said to go to her surgery tomorrow, look at teeth, see what do."

Wow! I felt a lump in my throat and such joy welling up in me as I said, "What a mighty, awesome, wonderful God we serve."

The question of healing

Do I pray for healing if people ask me? You pray for healing so automatically that, whether people ask for healing or not, you just pray for healing, because the Lord wants people healed! He doesn't want them sick. It's all so simple.

Chapter 3

Outreach in China with YWAM (1981, 1983 and 1988)

At the border checkpoint between the mainland of China and Hong Kong, I and seven other YWAM outreach members stood in pairs, waiting in line. The centres and sides of our holdalls were packed with small New Testaments printed in Chinese. Just ahead of us was the Chinese customs.

It was June 1981, China was still a very closed country, and carrying Bibles or New Testaments in was illegal. Yet our team of eight was attempting to take in small New Testaments to give out. We had paid US$50 each to enter as tourists. We and our hand luggage were searched in pairs. We were a bundle of nerves – who wouldn't be? The first couple got through... and so did their bags. The second pair also got through undetected. Halfway there!

Then it was the turn of the third couple. They passed through the barrier successfully, but the officials stopped them to search their bags. One woman customs official undid the central section of one of the bags, and there in full view were the New Testaments. Immediately, she and several other women customs officials started shouting and screaming their heads off, in Chinese presumably! I can recall my emotions – utter and complete grief and disappointment.

Those who had gone through already were called back. Now all our bags were searched, and the central section of each bag was emptied. But this was the amazing thing: the woman customs official who had found the New Testaments in the centre of a bag was so busy shouting at us that she didn't search the side sections.

The shouting continued, and we were told that we could pick up the little pocket-size books on our way out of the country. Despite all this, we were still allowed to enter China. So through we went, each of us amazed at how God had blinded the eyes of the customs officials. For there, in the sagging sides of our bags, were the other New Testaments which, despite the tell-tale shapes in the bags, had gone undetected!

Throughout the trip, we had to keep up the appearance of being tourists. As tourists, we had to visit a dam. We also spent time in Sheklung, which was poverty-ridden, with people sitting on the pavements selling their meagre wares of a crab or two, or a few vegetables. The railway platform was sickening, as it had been used as a public toilet. Today, so I understand, Sheklung is a glittering, high-rise, prosperous city, thanks to us Westerners all buying cheap Chinese goods. What a difference some twenty-five years can make.

Bags of opportunities

My second visit to China was in 1983 with a young YWAM colleague. Again the real purpose for which we had been sent across the border was to help smuggle in Bibles – a real cloak-and-dagger affair as the Chinese police were swooping on and imprisoning (or worse) Chinese couriers caught carrying Bibles for the "underground" and persecuted Christian communities.

Ron, my very tall American male co-worker, who was only 18 or 19 years old (and I felt so sorry for him), had to go and locate the bags filled with Bibles that had been left behind by previous couriers in the left-luggage areas of various Chinese hotels. We had been given cloakroom tickets and keys to collect them.

Ron had been gone for ages and ages, and I was getting very upset, sitting in one part of this huge Chinese hotel, wondering what had happened. But he arrived back safely with the bags, and we walked together from the hotel past Chinese police to a nearby agreed rendezvous, where we awaited the arrival of two 18-year-old Christian Chinese girls from Hong Kong. At first we missed the Chinese pair, but when we did meet up with them, they took us as their guests back into the Chinese hotel and into its traditional-style restaurant with grotesque figures on the wall. We had a lovely meal with them, bless their hearts!

Then they left with the bags which we had brought back into the hotel and had handed over to them. We all just walked out, amazed at how easily it had all happened. We did not know where the two girls were bound for, risking their lives to bring more copies of God's Word to China's underground churches, but Ron and I were glad to have been a link in a long and dangerous distribution chain. Even our small contribution had been a hair-raising experience.

Kid's stuff

My third visit to China in 1988 began, for reasons explained in Chapter 11, with an unintended double entry into the country! The Communist government would never knowingly have allowed in evangelists, and my first two visits with other members of YWAM had been in the role of tourists. For my third trip, I had a new 'cover story' – I was going to be part of a 'cultural friendship team'.

At this point, I need to give you a little background. I've been told that back in the early days after the Cultural Revolution, the Chinese authorities set up after-school activity centres, known as "Children's Palaces", where the children of working-class parents could study the arts. Initially encouraged by Chairman Mao, over the next 30 years they were created all over China, and continue to flourish.

The authorities were justifiably proud of these Children's Palaces, which offered these kids a tremendous range of activities – dance, choir, orchestra, drama, and puppets, to mention just a few. Every subject was taught, studied, and performed to the highest standard. By the 1980s, the authorities were ready to welcome "cultural friendship teams" from other countries. Surprise, surprise! There were Christians – children and some older folk – willing to wear that new label, and, in the case of the kids, fully able to put on a lively, entertaining, and evangelistic show! Enter King's Kids.

King's Kids International is a ministry of YWAM that works in partnership with families, churches, and other like-minded ministries, and welcomes all generations to its schools and outreaches. So a team of King's Kids going out on mission, as in the rest of this chapter and in other chapters of this book, would include older family members and other adults – like me – supporting them.

Back to the story. I met my King's Kids team in Beijing in September 1988. We were officially a cultural friendship team, so we were taken on a tour of some of the main Children's Palaces – these, as I've explained, were cultural centres. There we saw room after room filled with sweet-faced young boys and girls, learning all manner of arts, musical instruments, and dance, geared to earthly standards of perfection, but without expressing any emotion.

King's Kids were invited to perform in the palace. Despite the setting, the team produced 30 minutes of praise to God in songs, drama and dance with shining faces, dazzling smiles and joy. In contrast, the Chinese boys and girls followed with songs lasting a few minutes, sung with poker faces.

The most thrilling performance by our King's Kids was at The Great Wall before thousands of tourists. Despite the crowds constantly moving past us, a number stopped for conversations, leading in some cases to conversions, as we spent several hours there. What a privilege. I thank God for that open door.

We then took a 17-hour train journey to Shanghai. I, being 68 at the time, was chosen to share the night section of the journey with three male teenagers – an enlightening experience! No sleep, of course! In Shanghai, King's Kids took every opportunity to perform in parks, gardens, and even jade and ivory factories, as the workers asked us to demonstrate what we did! The Word surely went forth by any and all means.

And so, on to Hong Kong aboard the SS *Shanghai* – and another divine appointment! The ship's officers announced over the loudspeakers that there was to be a marathon concert where passengers could either perform or pay to be entertained. Yes, people paid US$20 to be presented with King's Kids praising God. I could hear the angels laughing.

Chapter 4

Outreach in Japan with YWAM
(1982, 1983 and 1985)

Even in a developed country such as Japan, there are many remote parts and thousands of scattered islands. As a result, Dr Oswald J Smith's challenge (based on Matthew 24:14) from an earlier era is still relevant: "If we want to bring back the King, we must take the Gospel to the last tribe, last people, last nation and the regions beyond where Christ has not been named."

So I would like to share some of the exciting things that the Lord did during the summer of 1982, when I went to join 300 or more others on a YWAM outreach in Japan – "Japan For Jesus". Some of us – including me – were sent out in twos to work with churches the length and breadth of Japan. My team-mate was a 21-year-old Canadian girl. We were sent first to Etajima, an island in the Japan Inland Sea, taking the Bullet Train from Tokyo to Hiroshima where the pastor from Etajima met us to take us to his island.

There are 3,400 islands in the Sea, and we went where Jesus had rarely, if ever, been made known before. We were joined by another team of three. Our hosting pastors humbly served us, while giving us almost all of the ministry.

Each day, on arrival at a new island, they would take us, complete with accordion, guitar, and PA system, around the whole place. We would invite and bring back many children to our boat to watch our performance and hear the gospel message. We went out again in the early evening to seek adults, and almost all who came responded to the gospel. It was surely time to reap His harvest there.

A number of experiences stand out of this time. On the island of Heigun, one lady whom we met was Oida, She was 77 years old and had been a Christian since her youth. She brought six old Buddhist ladies with her to a meeting to hear the gospel. They all received Jesus into their hearts because they had seen her joy and peace and wanted it for themselves.

These old Japanese know that, living on these islands, Shintoism is not the Way for them because there are no priests to bury them. This is why they are all "officially" Buddhist. One of the impressions that stayed with me from this outreach was that joy and peace were not to be found in either Shintoism or Buddhism.

I attended the wedding of a delightful couple and was amazed that they were not permitted to smile. I also went to a funeral, where there was a huge photo of the dead man to be left on his ashes, so that those visiting the site will know whose ashes they were, and remember to burn joss sticks for him.

In six days some 220 souls came into the kingdom. During this time, my team-mate Barbara and I were led by our pastor in a New Testament-type ministry, where we would call on people's homes, be invited in, eat, drink, share, pray, and invite to church, where some came and were saved. Praise God!

Back on the mainland, we saw the entire staff and girls in a home for unmarried mothers in Hiroshima respond to Jesus. Then it was time to leave for Osaka, where we were assigned to three 'sister churches' for the last three weeks. It was a different story there, as we were asked to weed gardens, clean churches, assemble tracts, and give them out door to door, as well as teach at ladies' meetings and preach in church. Being ministry to and in the church, it did not reap the same kind of fruit, but we saw the Lord move as His people were challenged to be His light in a dark land.

Return trip

Those precious pastors from the Inland Sea invited me to return anytime, so I went back in June 1983 before reporting to YWAM Hong Kong for six months' outreach with the Far Eastern Evangelistic Team (FEET). Once again, I had the incredible privilege of Holy Spirit-led door-to-door ministry, sharing, praying, preaching, eating, drinking, leading them to the Lord, or inviting them to church to hear more. This was in both Etajima and Kyushu. We saw God move in a home for girls who were pregnant or already mothers as a result of incest. How they needed – and responded to – love.

I was taken to a hospital in Hiroshima where victims of the atomic bomb were still suffering. They were skin and bone and were carried around in a net. I wept copious tears before asking forgiveness, but there was no response, as you can imagine, nearly 40 years after the event.

Saving and cleansing

My third visit to Japan was in the spring of 1985. I prayed for a partner and God gave me two – Valli from my home church and Maree from New Zealand who was in my home town of Crawley, Sussex, waiting for direction from God.

Our team of three met in Etajima as planned. On Easter Sunday we baptised four people in the sea and also sprinkled an 83-year-old lady. From then on, we were invited into home after home, where we ate (sometimes sumptuous meals centred around raw fish), sang and danced to worship songs, gave testimonies, and preached the gospel; the Lord graciously saving one by one. Every meeting ended in extensive prayer as we saw people healed physically and emotionally and delivered from bondages.

On one occasion, as a result of tracts being handed out, 24 young people came to a 9am Sunday School. Following our preaching, 14 asked Jesus to be their Lord. On our last day in that place, we left at 5am for a pastors' meeting in Hiroshima. We were asked to dance and speak. The Lord's presence was so powerful that the prayer time was spent in repentance. Nine pastors were so convicted that in repentance they wept before the Lord.

We then went on to three house meetings – times of praise and worship in people's homes – and finally at 7pm a battered wives home where six people received Jesus. We returned home at 11pm. Never has Philippians 4:13 – ***"I can do all things through Him who strengthens me"*** – been more real to me!

We travelled on to Kokura, in the south-east region of Kyushu. Once again, we had many house and church meetings. We attended pastors' 7am prayer meetings. At one, we danced and the Lord told me to tear up my notes and read Ezekiel 3:26-27:

> *"I will make your tongue stick to the roof of your mouth so that you will be silent and unable to rebuke them, though they are a rebellious house. But when I speak to you, I will open your mouth and you shall say to them, 'This is what the Sovereign Lord says: "Whoever will listen, let him listen, and whoever will refuse, let him refuse, for they are a rebellious house."'"*

Phew! He spoke, but this time I did not witness a repentant spirit, though each of the pastors prayed.

Each Saturday afternoon we ministered in the park, and each week our pastor expected a new programme for this time. God was faithful, as always.

One Sunday in Kokura Castle was particularly memorable. After we danced and sang, a man came and asked for prayer because he was about to kill himself. He had even written his suicide note. Instead, he received a new life in Jesus. Before we left, a group of break-dancers gave us their spot where they had been dancing all day and the use of their speakers for our worship tape. Hundreds of people heard as we danced. It is all easy when the Lord leads.

We gave out tracts. We spoke at a junior high school to over 1,000 girls, and then to a college where around 300 heard the message. No salvation calls were permitted, but we were able to make a challenge to "consider Jesus".

These are just some of the stories as the Lord went with us to save, heal, and deliver. Two of our pastors are now with the Lord, another has faithfully corresponded for 17 years. One day it will be TIME for Japan. The Lord showed me in 1974, when I saw Japanese people all over the world, that, when HIS time comes, they will GO wherever God says, not to sightsee but for HIS GLORY.

No-one can speak of Japan without mentioning their baths, both in houses and the communal bathhouses. I love them, with their sense of cleansing, relaxing, and (in the communal case) socialising. The other unforgettable but not-so-enjoyable experience was my visit to the *Kabuki* Theatre in Tokyo. Hour after hour of beauty, horror, life, and death. Some folk sleep, many eat their noodles – or whatever – from cardboard boxes, with chopsticks of course. To the uninitiated, it's a matter of leaving through fatigue, or hunger, or both.

Chapter 5

Korea – visit to Prayer Mountain and a prison (1982)

When you are out on an outreach in a faraway country, sometimes it is good to take the opportunity to visit somewhere else. So, following 'Japan For Jesus' in September 1982, I made a personal visit to Seoul, Korea, to visit Senior Pastor David (Paul) Yonggi Cho's Yoido Full Gospel Church and Fasting Prayer Mountain.

On arrival, a Pastor Lee (one of many pastors named Lee that I met there!) greeted me. As we passed a "Yoido Prayer Mountain" sign I said three words, "Britain needs this." He did not comment, but escorted me to a prayer cell, small enough only to sit. This was where I planned to spend two days. I settled in to pray and listen to what God would say.

Imagine my amazement when, an hour later, someone knocked at my door! I opened the small entrance to my prayer cell and there was Pastor Lee again. He said, "Come." I said, "Where?" He repeated, "Come," so I climbed out. He said, "You speak." I said, "What? Where?" He led me to a large tent called *Ephesus* – one of the huge tents (the others were called *Antioch* and *Jerusalem*) that housed the church services while the church building was being built.

The pastor opened the tent flap, and I entered. Shock! Thousands of Koreans were waiting. I walked up the blue velvet carpeted stairs, but rapidly descended again as Pastor Lee indicated that I was still wearing my shoes! Hurriedly removing them, I said, "What am I supposed to say?" He replied, "What you said as you came in – Britain needs this." "Oh, okay, I can do that," I replied.

Looking out onto the audience of many thousands, I launched into a brief history of how the British took Jesus to many Asian nations, but now were in need of Jesus and their own Prayer Mountain. A roar went up and the pastor said, "Thank you – okay." I said, "Not okay, they pray now."

He told them to pray, and a noise like nothing I have heard before or since broke forth. The man immediately in front of me soaked his shirt in seconds crying to God for Britain! The small tinkling bell was rung and amazingly penetrated the noise so that complete silence reigned. I waved goodbye, descended the stairs, put on my shoes, went back to my cell, and praised God at the top of my voice for what He had done.

So, what did God say to me during my time in the cell? I knew that dear YWAM friends had been taking a *Toymaker* team to different nations. (*Toymaker* is a drama which covers the Bible story from Creation to the Resurrection.) God said that I was to go to Pusan and join them; the drama was wonderful, but the word of salvation must also be preached.

I went to the church office to enquire about how I could get to Pusan. The lady working there told me, "Bus, long way, when you go?" I said, "Friday." She looked shocked as she said, "It's all-night prayer, people come here on Fridays by boat, train, bus, and plane, and this week is very special with televised communion – and you go?" I said, "Yes, God said." Needless to say, I only had enough money for a single fare and did not, of course, have an address.

A real drama

I got off the bus and took a taxi into the centre of Pusan. One member of the *Toymaker* team was idly looking out from the garden of the beautiful house, high on a hill, that someone had allowed them to live in while they were in Pusan. He saw me getting out of the taxi, shouted to the others, and ran to find me, which he did.

He took me to the house where we had a joyful reunion. The next day, the team gave a performance of *Toymaker* in the garden of the house, which was well attended. After this, I had some in-depth discussions on salvation with three Korean men.

That evening, Kevin, my friend and the team leader, said, "Florence, we are going to a boys' prison tomorrow. Would you like to come along?" I said, "Yes." Upwards of 300 boys aged between 18 and 21 years were present. As the drama was about to commence, Kevin said that the Lord had told him I was to speak after the performance. This I did, using their translator.

A strong call was made, but nobody responded. I thought that the fear of man had stopped them, so began to pray, entreating God to save those who were His. Rebuking the fear of man, I quoted that we need to fear Him who can destroy both soul and body, not those who can only kill the body (Matt 10:28). What I had not realised was that the translator was translating this! A further call was made and two-thirds of the young men stood up to commit their lives to Jesus.

After a time of worship together with the Korean believers who had joined us there, newly-converted believers turned towards the boys who had not responded and sang, "We love you with the love of the Lord". I wept, as did others. The angels rejoiced, and all the glory goes to God who does all things well. By the way, my friends gave me a gift which paid for my journey back to Seoul. Praise the Lord!

Aeroplane appointment

On the plane back to Tokyo I found myself sitting next to a young Japanese man. He opened up the conversation by telling me his name. That morning I had asked the Lord, as I usually did, for divine appointments and conversations. However, my flight had been delayed for several hours and I was feeling the fatigue of many weeks of mission, so I chose to cut him off by burying my face behind a newspaper. Soon it was mealtime and I bowed my head in thanksgiving. That is when the Holy Spirit said, "You choose to ignore the appointment that you asked the Lord for." Penitent, I turned to Noboku and apologised, telling him my name. He asked what I had been doing in Korea so I told him, plus most of the good news when, horror, it was landing time!

It was 11.30pm in the airport, and soon there was nobody around but us. Noboku still wanted to hear more. His last bus went at midnight so finally he had to go. I said, "Please pray to ask Jesus into your life." He nodded affirmation and ran. I said, "O Lord, now I don't know if he does it or not." The Lord replied with, I thought, a smile: "If you had started at the beginning you would have known the end." What a merciful God we have.

Postscript

There is now a World Prayer Centre in Birmingham and a Prayer House for England on the Ugandan Prayer Mountain, very similar to the Yoido Prayer Mountain. Many thousands from many nations go to these venues to pray. The Lord answers prayer in His perfect timing.

Chapter 6

Outreach in Thailand with YWAM (1983)

All my senses were aroused. My FEET team of 24 was taking a train from Malaysia into Thailand. On every platform were rows of Buddhist priests in their orange robes; vendors balanced their delicacies on their heads while gesticulating with their hands and arms; and wherever I looked there were individual small dishes of unknown foods and large dishes of green vegetables with small fish. Inside the train, every table was decorated with deep pink orchids in a vase.

Bangkok was chaos as cars, bikes, and rickshaws vied for space. The roads were crammed with people. Flower markets were a festoon of colour and perfumes. Plastic bags, filled with water or juice and with a straw attached, were greatly in demand. Thai edifices – a riot of colour whether shrines or palaces – delighted the eye, as did the Thai people, so gentle and gracious.

Our accommodation was quite a way out of town. We walked with our trainers tied round our necks for most of our ten days there, as torrential rain caused the water level on the roads to be up to our knees.

Members of a church joined us as we went to shopping centres and the red-light district where 'go-go' bars, pimps, and prostitutes mingled alongside street vendors selling food and drink. My heart went out to small girls, abroad half the night, selling flowers. It went out to the bigger girls too, plying their trade. Some were deeply moved as we talked with them about a loving God who died for them. We were able to pray, sing, dance, and preach right outside the bars, watched by many without interference.

Two dumb boys selling goods heard the gospel and silently asked Jesus into their lives. I rebuked the dumb spirit and their tongues were loosed. They said, in both English and Thai, "Jesus is my Lord!" Glory to God!

People were invited to attend a church to hear more. The following Sunday, 26 of those whom we invited responded to the gospel. That church was greatly encouraged, for which we praised God.

Chapter 7

Outreach in India with YWAM (1983)

*"Him who is holy and true...
what He opens, no-one can shut, and
what He shuts, no-one can open..."*
Revelation 3:7

What a huge, fascinating, dangerous, yet beautiful land India is. Words cannot convey the initial sensory shock when our FEET Team, mentioned in the previous chapter, arrived in Calcutta on a 13-week mission in October 1983. Streets packed with people, dodging buses, taxis, cars, trams, dogs, sacred cows, and countless rickshaws, pulled by running men; children washing their naked bodies from a running tap in the gutter. Yet after a few days I loved this city. The market was amazing with fish, meat, fruit, and vegetables on sale beside lamps, clothes, and household goods of every kind. The live chickens looked half-dead, but the people were vibrantly alive.

Our team of 24 included five Indians. We lived at an orphanage for boys with 60 residents who, like us, had to vacate the classrooms where we had been sleeping by 6am daily – to make room for the day students! After an early breakfast, our bags had to be packed and stored in a cupboard. When – inevitably – someone was sick, they had to stay in the cupboard with water to drink and a spare door to lie on, until the day students departed at 4pm.

However, it was a great outreach. We preached in parks, including Victoria Park, where we were often escorted out by police, as Hindus and Muslims entered into disputes between themselves.

One day, while preaching, I saw a lady who was obviously from the West taking many photos of our group. I was annoyed and was about to ask her to stop when I heard that it was Melody Green, recently widowed following the death of her husband Keith in a plane crash. She had come to visit us with the FEET Team director to give us some 'treats', which included showers and hair-washing in their respective rooms of their hotel. Then we were invited to dinner and couldn't help laughing when one team member found a cockroach in his rice in this 'posh' hotel.

Drops in the ocean

One morning, I arose at 4.30am to visit a feeding centre run by a man called Mark Buntain. Here, meals were prepared daily for 18,000 people. I was able to put my arms around many destitute mums and children, telling them that it's Jesus who loves them, feeds them, and died for them. What a wonderful work that was. Back then. it had been going for 25 years and, I trust, still is, though Mark is with the Lord. If love never fails, as the Bible says in 1 Corinthians 13:7, these people have all been touched by the love of God.

The hardest thing for me in Calcutta was walking past young men lying on the pavement in a foetal position and clearly dying. When I asked our Indian host why someone couldn't take them to hospital, I was told that the hospitals would only take in paying patients. That's when I understood the work of Mother Teresa, one of whose ministries was to send a vehicle round every morning to pick up the 'destitute and dying' so that they might receive love and comfort during their last hours on earth. She had other ministries too, rescuing discarded babies and caring for the 'sick and destitute'.

Later, I had the pleasure of meeting her and asked her what she thought she had achieved in her time there. She replied, "My work is a drop in the ocean, but then the ocean is made up of drops." Such humility! How India needs those drops.

What grieved me most was the endless *puja* (Hindu ceremonial offerings) complete with fire-crackers, elaborate floats with images of the gods of that caste, and a city with millions of lights permanently blazing. I think of the cost of these when so many people are poverty-stricken.

I remember, over 20 years later, two big brown eyes in a beautiful but very dirty face surrounded by a tangled mass of dark curls. I smiled at this girl but, terrified, she disappeared. Home for her was at best a *bustee* – a rough shelter made of any bit of material, tin, plastic, or wood. I had been astonished that there was no rubbish bin or collection in Calcutta, until I understood that nothing was thrown away. The biscuits that I purchased were wrapped in a large leaf. Paper is a luxury.

I did not see that little girl again, but I did see the untouchables and their *puja*.. Several poor, thin children were sitting on the back end of a wooden trolley with one hand of green bananas on the front. They were heading for the sea where the 'gift' would be tipped into the sea as an offering to their god. These children needed that food more than their god!

Around the big hotels were the professional beggars who used deliberately-maimed children for financial gain. Bigger boys were lying in the middle of horrendous traffic, a bowl on their stomachs, risking their lives for money. No wonder that the Bible says that the love of money is the root of all evil (1 Tim 6:10).

Speaking the same language

We performed many times in huge schools with hundreds of pupils using song, dance, drama, puppets, testimonies, and preaching. There was a wonderful response, and churches saw an increase in their numbers.

It is an amazing task to pastor in India. I remember seeing signs saying, "Bible study in Hindi, Gujarat, Bengali, Tamil or Urdu". Phew! Speaking of languages, I was the only British person on that team who saw the need to gently point out to our American FEET Team leaders that these children were educated under the British system, and words such as "cookies", "candies", and "trash" needed to be changed to "biscuits", "sweets", and "rubbish" if the sketches were to be understood.

The Lord deals with us as we 'go'. One day, an 18-year-old Canadian girl had a picture of someone standing on a high diving board, going through preparatory movements before making a difficult dive. Coming up in the water, the Lord was there, and He said, "I only wanted you to jump into My arms from the side." When she gave that picture, I knew that I was that diver and have never forgotten that He loves us for who we are, not what we do.

By the way, we ate rice and *dahl* daily, so most of our young men, without their usual steak diet, saw their muscles disappear during the three months we spent in India. I was put in charge of finance, which proved to be a nightmare as we needed to change big banknotes daily to hand out to our small teams going to different places. And then we had to get them to account for the money at the end of the day!

So ended my India visit. I have been invited back several times, but the door has always been closed. The scripture quoted at the beginning of this chapter tells us who has closed it, and I am so grateful that He leads and guides if we ask Him to – bless His Holy Name!

Chapter 8

Outreach at the Olympic Games, USA, with YWAM (1984)

O ur God moves in amazing ways! One such occasion was how He used a visit to Wales to open the door for me to participate in the 1984 summer Olympic Games Christian Outreach in Los Angeles.

I had made an enquiry about the outreach, and YWAM had told me that their teams were already made up and a plane had been chartered, but that I could join them if I could get to Los Angeles. However, I found out that airline staff travel to Los Angeles and surrounding cities was banned all summer by all major airlines; this ban also affected those like me who could normally fly on a stand-by basis for just ten per cent of the normal fare.

So on this occasion I needed big funds to pay for tickets and fees. Meanwhile, I was asked to speak at a meeting in Wales. At the end of the meeting I met a young lady who said, "Until today I was going with YWAM to the Olympic Games, but this morning the Lord said, 'You failed your exams. You need to stay at home and study this summer.' He also told me to accompany my mother to this meeting, which I normally never do!" She then asked me if I thought she would get her money back. I said, "Yes, because I'm taking your place."

She was delighted and gave me an immediate gift of her £75 deposit. My church, recognising that God was moving in this situation, gave me a generous gift and agreed to cover the remaining £625 until the Lord brought it in. All I had to do was pack and depart on 20 July. Needless to say, the money came in almost immediately.

Running the race

Olympic Games are a great source of statistics and stories. Here are a few from the 1984 Olympics that you won't often hear quoted.

Over 11,000 Christian workers came from 77 nations. Of these, 7,000 were on teams recruited by 22 different Christian organisations. In addition, 4,000 worked in arts and entertainment, giving over 700 hours of presentations in 1,000 locations spread over 80 miles!

Millions of pieces of literature were distributed in several languages. Spiritual and physical needs were met in crisis centres, drop-in shelters, and soup kitchens. Some prayer cells had prayed for one year over every street in that huge city. A torch had been carried 3,400 miles through 18 US states. Groups were praying even in Korea.

What was the result? People were saved on the beaches, in parks, and at every venue. Upwards of 12,000, so I was told.

My team was assigned low-key jobs; the Lord was busy character-building, dealing with jealousy, independent spirits, and lack of long-suffering, to name just a few areas which community life tests. God's first concern is our relationship with Him. I just worked along with those the Lord gave me, but He did have one enormous blessing, which happened when I was sent, with a partner, to the main athletics arena.

After a lot of one-to-one evangelism, during which a Mexican lady and her seven children had prayed for salvation, my partner and I went to the exit. Almost immediately a man came down the steps with his son. He asked, "Would you like our tickets? We have to leave now."

We were due for a half-hour tea break, so we agreed. We mounted endless steps, for even though we had US$60 tickets, our seats were quite high up. Imagine my joy and amazement when they announced the next race: the final event of the decathlon – the 1,500 metres, which would decide if the British athlete Daley Thompson would win the gold medal or not. He did, and we, having eaten our packed tea, left rejoicing and praising God for the blessing of the seats for just that moment.

Post-Games...

Most of the British outreach team went home straight after the Games finished. Some of the team, however, felt led to stay on for another three weeks. I was one of them. This was the Lord's time to answer my prayer to increase me in serving and mercy ministry. We all worked on rebuilding a hotel that, for a time, became home to Mercy Ships people, including my own daughter who at that time was running the ship's bank single-handedly – together with the Lord!

We distributed food to the poor, and went on outreach in the evenings into gay bars, discos, or wherever the Spirit led. I also had the opportunity to speak to one huge congregation about abortion. It should have been our male leader who spoke, but he thought I could deal with it more forcefully. I categorically stated that it is murder and in the ensuing fellowship time found myself being attacked (verbally) by militant pro-choice Christians! May the Lord speak to us all on these matters.

Chapter 9

Outreach in Tonga with YWAM (1987)

"But you will receive power when the Holy Spirit comes on you; and you will be my witnesses in Jerusalem, and in all Judea and Samaria, and to the ends of the earth." Acts 1:8

The South Pacific is so beautiful – azure seas, coral reefs, palm trees, and myriads of stars. This was one of the blessings of nine weeks of mission devoted to the Tongan Islands. There were also many trials and minor tribulations, as there usually are in missions…

It was spring 1987, and I was one of three staff leading 20 YWAM DTS students and one Tongan interpreter on outreach to nine of the 38 Tongan islands. Our goal was to establish contact so that teams could visit in the future.

We travelled by aircraft large and small, a barge, and a 65-foot yacht called *Amazing Grace*, crewed by New Zealanders. We also had to use rubber dinghies to traverse the lethal reefs, which had kept intruders away for centuries. For that, we travelled one passenger at a time in dinghies paddled by an islander. Some Tongan islanders had not seen a white man for years, if at all.

Of puppets and kings

We ministered through puppetry, drama, testimonies, and preaching in schools, and in a hospital where we prayed for the sick; but mainly we held 'open airs'. These were different, in that Tongans didn't have watches and don't live by 'time' as we in the West do! We gathered at the Morris Hedstrum Warehouse – the place where everyone went to buy everything – and began to sing. Within an hour or so there was quite a crowd.

The people loved our puppets, which are such a great means for communicating the gospel, and our Bible stories. "The Prodigal Son" caused many to find Jesus. The "Laughing Song" had them rolling in the grass. And the children adored the strange puppet creatures singing "Jesus loves the little children".

We even performed for the king, which was exciting. (I have heard that he became a believer later in life.) At that time protocol decreed that no-one's head was to be higher than his. Since he was lying on a *chaise-longue*, his equerry and staff had to crouch when approaching him.

Island reflections

Tongan lives in 1987 were old-fashioned, more like my idea of England a century ago. Some islands we visited had no cars, phones, or electricity. Fresh water was in short supply and only for drinking. We had to wash our clothes and ourselves in salt water.

The people 'farm' their area of bush, growing oranges, bananas, yams, watermelons, and sweet potatoes. Coconut palms are everywhere. The people live in huts made of palm fronds, surrounded by dogs, pigs, chickens, or goats. Many men smoke and drink *kava*, a potent drink made from palm roots. The islands produce fruit which is delicious and sweet – but disgusting to look at. The bananas are double-barrelled like binoculars or triangular in shape, the oranges are brown.

Tongan men wear skirts but, being mostly huge, they look manly in what we regard as women's apparel. Women, on the other hand, are not supposed to show a leg. So we women guests swam in long skirts and tops with modest necklines – and never swam on Sundays! It is probably still so for many Tongans today.

Tongans are beautiful but also very religious. This religiosity had its seeds back in 1885, when two Swedish missionaries went to Tonga Tapu, the main island. The then-king favoured one of the missionaries, asking him to establish the Church of Tonga, and ignored the other missionary. With the Tongan Church born in division, many have fallen away from the Truth and become religious. Church bells ring all day on Sundays, and Tongans, dressed in their best – whether appropriate or not – rush to church. While attending the Sunday services, I observed that, once the hymn-singing was over, many appeared to be asleep, waking only in time to leave. No-one stayed to speak with or greet one another.

On one island called Lifonga, it was different. Our translator came from there. He not only knew everyone but was also, it seemed, related to all of them! We saw what 'extended family' means: they are obliged to provide and care for each other. We joined them for 5.30am prayers every morning, and participated in their Sunday services. When we left, the entire population came to sing farewell with tears. They gave us whole stalks of bananas, and made *leis* (similar to the garlands of flowers made famous in Honolulu) for all the team from the island's glorious flowers. We sailed away on the *Amazing Grace*. Several of us took turns at the wheel in this vast expanse of beautiful but rough blue sea.

Learning curve

At one point, my team was left on Uifa, a group of little-known islands. We walked everywhere. The beaches were stunning. I collected amazing seashells, battered small pieces of white shell with a hole in each. The seashells were more or less circular, and my two granddaughters back in England have made lovely necklaces using them.

Uifa was also where I had wildly differing but instructive experiences. One day, I decided to swim across a small stretch of water to another island. Halfway across, I realised that I was being carried backwards while swimming forwards! Happily, one of the men on our team was a lifeguard from California. He helped me to get ashore, but chastised me for attempting to swim across that channel. How humiliating – and didn't I deserve it!

On another island, I made a bad cultural mistake. We were sleeping in the chief's house, and as an honoured guest I was watched over by three ladies all night. For the first two nights, I did not sleep a wink. Enough! I said to myself and, picking up my sleeping bag, went to the Nissen hut where the men were sleeping and slept soundly, despite pounding rain on the corrugated roof. Sadly, it was obvious that my action had caused offence, and my apology was not understood. Since then I have read some wonderful books, emphasising how important it is to understand different cultures and not try to change them, as missionaries invariably used to do. God has been, and is, using the cultures of many islands to worship Him.

After one church service, the minister's wife invited me to lunch. What took place astounded me. We could not sit until the minister did. His son sat opposite me and his wife served all three of us. The minister never addressed a word to me – he just gobbled his food and left. His son informed me that I was privileged to sit at his father's table because he supervised 17 Methodist churches on different islands and was a Very Important Person. I said that my Father was even more important, being omnipotent, omniscient, and omnipresent. The son made no reply and left.

Then the wife and I ate, and I spoke with her about 1 Corinthians 3, where it says that our work will be tested by fire. I used my ring to explain that the precious stone will not burn, but that their homes of wood and rushes would. She understood, wept, and prayed with me for her salvation, once again revealing our wonderful God of the individual.

Chapter 10

Outreach to Utah Mormons with YWAM (1986, 1987 and 1988)

Sweat rolled down my back and forehead. My wooden burden was digging into my shoulder. The sun beat down on the road I was walking. I've done some crazy things for God in my time, but carrying an eight-foot wooden cross for miles and miles was certainly one of the most physically demanding.

It was June 1986, and God had called me to carry a cross around Salt Lake City, the state capital of Utah in the USA and the centre of the Mormon Church. My friend Frank Gobel from the USA had also received such a call. We met in Salt Lake City for YWAM's Summer of Mission. While the eight-foot-high cross with a wheel at the bottom end was being made, we attended and evangelised at the Manti Pageant. This is a huge spectacle depicting first the failure of the Christian Church, followed by the whole Mormon saga. There were huge banners saying, "Christians are here! Don't talk to them."

The time came to carry the cross, so I joined Frank and two other men to do the carrying. On the first day, the Lord gave me the supernatural strength to walk 30 miles, all four of us took turns to carry the cross around the city perimeter. The next day, the two other men dropped out, literally muscle-bound. Frank and I, joined by others, walked the last 12 miles in teeming rain. It was a standard raised against the powers of darkness, not against human beings.

A few days later, a team of Christian deaf carried the cross seven times around the Salt Lake City Temple. What a glorious silent witness, as they sang with their hands. It was a privilege to walk with them.

On the night of 23 July we all went into the city to join the thousands sleeping on the pavements awaiting the annual Mormon parade of 240 floats, which lasts nearly four hours. Many conversations took place before, during, and after the parade. I walked up and down the street before the event proclaiming 1 Corinthians 1:18:

"For the message of the cross is foolishness to those who are perishing, but to us who are being saved it is the power of God."

I felt that the angels were applauding. We had some definite results too: Ed Decker, an American evangelist, baptised three ex-Mormons in the jacuzzi in the Sheraton Hotel. To God be the glory.

A different learning curve

The following August (1987) I was drawn back to Utah for another YWAM Summer of Mission. Our team of eight went off to visit the Mormon missionary centre in Provo. At the entrance was a board with the names, at that time, of 31 languages. You chose the one you wanted to learn and from that moment on only communicated in it. Such efficiency, devotion, discipline, and commitment amazed me – we can certainly learn things from other faiths, even if we don't agree with their beliefs.

We visited the missionary centre's library and saw their culture leaflets (dos and don'ts), of which I took a few – invaluable to carry around in your Bible if you are called to many nations, as I have been – and to help avoid the sort of cultural mistakes I had made that same year in Tonga.

We then went into a meeting where two young men were telling how they had learnt Spanish in two months and their imminent departure for Colombia. Then it was question time. First, one of our team asked them why they said they knew the book of Mormon was the truth because of the burning in their breast. We countered with Luke 24:32 when "hearts burned" because Jesus spoke explaining the scriptures. At the second question, the police came to escort us out!

A King's Kids team from Hawaii came to Salt Lake City to join us. They were aged from three to 19 and powerfully presented song, dance, and testimonies. They also prayed for people – including us. A five-year-old boy prayed for me and I felt the love of God pour over me. The Lord opened my eyes to see the plight of children as the King's Kids told of how Satan attacks them through games, books, toys, music, and TV. The enemy has tried to kill children from the beginning and is still trying by all means. We adults need to pray for their protection. I believe the Lord will use children even more powerfully before Jesus returns.

Among the Mormons

The time had come to go out in teams. My co-leader was a 28-year-old mountaineer. We ranged in age from 16 to 66; only seven of us, but from four different nations.

Much was accomplished. We drove north into Idaho, then south into Arizona: I slept in 14 beds, including a tent, the team van when the ground was flooded, a settee, a Gortex mountain sleeping bag, and a proper bed. Walking over 150 miles, we carried a cross approximately 20 miles around another three of the six Mormon temples, smothered towns with 20,000 donated copies of a book called *The Mormon Illusion*, and briefly visited another seven towns which were too spread out for door-to-door visiting. We had conversations with upwards of 5,000 Mormons. Thousands of tracts were handed out, plus 2,160 books. Some Mormons were aggressive because we were there – yet they send young men and women into all the world and boast of huge conquests.

There were lighter moments too. In Zion National Park in Utah, it was hilarious trying to get food before the squirrels got it. They ate a hole in my handbag in their search for food, and in my friend Kim's shorts to get her M&M sweets. Then, adding insult to injury, they used our tent as a toilet or restroom – or whatever you call it.

One of our team was George, a high-ranking prince from the Solomon Islands. He looked so fierce. At one campsite a group of boys were constantly watching us. One night, George sat up in his sleeping bag, revealing a very black face and fuzzy hair with a red comb in it. The group of boys shrieked and ran for their lives from this gentle giant.

The most incredible encounter was Colorado City, Arizona, where we came across a community following the doctrines of Brigham Young, who led the early Mormon pioneers after Joseph Smith (the founder of the Mormon Church) was murdered in jail in 1844. The traditional early Mormon invitation was "Come in with your all." This seemed to boil down to: Give them your money; work for the community; marry as directed ("As many wives as you like – we practise polygamy here."); and old-fashioned (Victorian) clothes and hairstyles (no trousers for women, nor even shorts for children). It seemed impossible to leave – unless you were prepared to walk out into the desert with nothing.

I felt so sad. They are beautiful people who need love, prayer, and salvation. Satan certainly is the deceiver, and there are many who are being deceived. Jesus said,

> *"I am the way and the truth and the life. No-one comes to the Father except through me."*

All the great religions believe that He was without sin, so He is not lying. Glory to the Lamb who is returning as a Lion!

ENCAPSULATING TWENTY-TWO YEARS OF MINISTRY

Florence in
Etijimia, Japan.

Florence celebrating
her 81st birthday
aboard the *Anastasis*.

Florence with the *Anastasis'* dental clinic volunteer crew in Eastern Europe.

Florence with the *Anastasis'* dental clinic volunteer crew in Eastern Europe.
Six ladies received the Lord that day.

Florence taking her turn carrying the eight foot wooden cross in Utah, USA.

Florence preaching in a market place in Lome, Togo. (1991).

Florence celebrating her 81st birthday, in Mauritania.

Florence in the *Revelation TV* studio after being
interviewed by David Falkus in July, 2004.

Chapter 11

YWAM Conference in the Philippines (1988)

C razy Jeepneys everywhere, painted in many different colours and most, if not all, carrying religious slogans. If I had a favourite people, it would be the Filipinos. They crowd the parks and stadiums to hear about God. Sadly, they are also subject to a lot of religiosity and false beliefs, but when the truth is preached, they receive it with joy and are willing to "go". These days, there are Filipinos in many Muslim nations, risking deportment, prison and even death. When I was in Morocco in 1999, King Hassan I was employing 18 Filipinos, who served in every lowly capacity. One exceptional lady was the King's interior decorator!

When it rains in Manila, many homes are flooded, yet the Filipinos come out impeccably dressed, looking for all the world as if they had just purchased their blouses and skirts. Stockings and high-heeled shoes defy the rain and mud. God is truly revered in the Philippines.

In September 1988, YWAM held a staff and leadership conference there. The opening and closing ceremonies featured performances from 300 members of King's Kids in six teams from several nations. I was 'staff', with a team of three-to-18-year-olds from Honolulu. Among the conference staff was my daughter Francine and her husband, David. They had no idea I was there. I watched them arrive, casually walked over and said "Hi." You can imagine their faces. "Mummy! What are you doing here?" said Francine. We had a great time together. There have been other such divine appointments in different nations. It shows me how much God loves me, and that's why I love Him.

Because our team had some very young members, we visited a number of huge primary schools. One had 1,800 children, who came and went in groups during our very long programme. We also went to homeless children and to a school in Balut which the 'rubbish-dump children' attended. Having fervently interceded for them, much seed was sown and the sick healed, especially from respiratory and digestive problems. It was a fruitful nine days.

Back and forth

WARNING! Only read this next bit
if you believe in a God of the Impossible…

At the end of my time in the Philippines, I needed to leave the evening before the rest of the team, as the airline had told me "No seats available for the next day" and I was on a concessionary ticket.

My plane landed in China. My visa was checked okay, but we were grounded because of horrendous rains, and I couldn't take the next leg of my journey to Beijing. The duty officer said, "Patience, we can't leave yet" to the grumbling passengers. Finally, after four hours, he announced that Beijing Airport was flooded and we must return to Manila!

I needed faith then, as I had no Filipino money, and whereas airlines will put passengers in hotels and feed them, this privilege is not usually extended to concessionary travellers like myself. I prayed hard. On arrival back in Manila, I was directed onto a bus which drove to the same hotel I had been in the first night, where I was given the same room as my daughter had been in – and vouchers for dinner and breakfast too!

The next morning, we were returned to the airport and boarded first. There were the King's Kids, waiting for their flight. They waved and shouted, "Florence, you left last night!" I said, "Yes, I've been to China and back, going again now. See you there." What a mighty God we serve, always doing wonders.

Chapter 12

Outreach in Barbados and Grenada with YWAM (1988)

"It was he who gave some to be apostles, some to be prophets, some to be evangelists, and some to be pastors and teachers, to prepare God's people for the equipping of the saints." Eph 4:11-12 KJV

The Lord had laid the Caribbean on my heart at the 1984 Olympics in Los Angeles. I've been asked how He did that, but I just had a strong feeling which I believed the Lord had given me. Three and a half years later, I received a brochure that proclaimed, ***"Answer the Call – Caribbean '88!"*** So I did.

Dual ministry

First came Barbados, a beautiful, small, coral island surrounded by sparkling blue sea, where, among the many species, one might see flying fish. At that time, 70 per cent of the population were Anglicans, who all dressed for Sunday church as though they were off to a wedding. The children had elaborate hairstyles, and satin or lace dresses with white stockings. They looked gorgeous.

My accommodation was with a Lebanese Christian family – a blessing indeed. I was asked to work with a YWAM School Of Evangelism outreach team from New Hampshire, USA. We were assigned to a large church, and reported at 8am for praise, worship, and spiritual warfare, before ministering to all age groups. It was very rewarding as many churchgoers were saved, healed, or delivered.

Counselling is not easy anywhere in the Caribbean, because so many women have several children by different fathers. Many are left to raise them with no man around, or a current man who is not the husband or father. ("Is this another legacy from the slave trade?" I asked myself.)

After ten days we moved to an even bigger church, and went from exciting people ministry to exciting practical ministry, as we were asked to paint the huge church building in four days. They wanted it ready for a crusade. At this point, I asked the Lord, "What now? This team have all their dramas, dances and puppets ready to work with this crusade?" But we painted the building as requested – and even had opportunity to use our dances, dramas, and the puppets in the church's outreach.

Shortly after, I was asked to pray about going over to Grenada to teach about evangelism in various churches around the island. The Lord confirmed through His Word in Ephesians 4:12 that evangelists are there "to equip the saints for the work". With the painting task completed, I left for Grenada.

Fruit in Grenada

Grenada: a lush, wild, beautiful volcanic island, in which spices, banana trees, and citrus fruit trees grow, without much help from man. The dominant religion is Catholicism. Though the island is fairly small, back in the late 1980s any journey took a lot of time as the atrocious roads were full of holes. Also, many huge plantations with 'great houses' were still operating. YWAM was renting one of these great houses.

I had been appointed to speak at six meetings in churches spread around the island. In-between weekends, I was to address around 150 people from three teams from Texas, Belize, and Jamaica. All these meetings brought repentance and recommitments. The Lord gave me words of knowledge for individuals, bringing freedom and deliverance. One-to-one prophecies brought healing, comfort, or encouragement. These teams included children and were powerful, as they 'blitzed' 12 towns, working in schools and churches, as well as large open-air meetings. Here are a few of the stories from that time.

A Texan man who was partially paralysed from five years of age was freed in the name of Jesus from the spirit of fear that had entered him at that time. Further prayer for a short leg caused it to lengthen. He was encouraged to exercise it, and the last I saw of him, he was walking four miles from the YWAM centre while I was being driven back to my lodgings.

Roger, the faithful driver for the YWAM centre, had great rings on the skin of his arms. I said, "What's that?" He replied, "Ringworm." I rebuked it in the name of Jesus, and the next day it was gone.

A 24-year-old Jamaican man with a bad stammer asked for prayer. First, the spirit of fear was cast out, as the Holy Spirit showed me that fear abounded among the West Indians as a result of ancestral slavery. The deaf and dumb spirit was told, in the name of Jesus, to go, and the man's speech immediately improved. A week later, he was still delighted with the improvement.

Hermie was a pastor's wife. She was a beautiful young mother of three, who asked for prayer because of trouble in her marriage. As soon as the spirit of jealousy was addressed, it left her with loud shrieks. This tearful lady said that her uncle had abused her and then told her that she was "no good". Glorious freedom came as various strongholds were broken. She renounced self-pity and the Lord's love washed over her, bringing healing, and cleansing.

After I had returned home, the YWAM Grenada leadership sent me a letter, saying that it had been a very fruitful time for the kingdom of God for both Grenadians and the teams. I do thank God and give Him all the glory for "a great door for effective ministry" (1 Cor 16:9) that He opened. To God be the glory. He did great things.

Chapter 13

Outreach in Jamaica with Mercy Ships (1988 and 1989)

"The harvest is passed and the summer over and you are not yet saved."

Jeremiah 8:20

I'm an evangelist. So you can understand that I was excited at the prospect of YWAM sending GO (Global Outreach) Teams to visit Bombay, Hong Kong, Tokyo, Manila, and finally Seoul, South Korea, for the 1988 Olympic Games. Wow! I thought, How exciting! What an opportunity!

To my surprise, the Lord told me to read Acts chapter 16. It's the story of Paul and Silas travelling north-west through much of what is now Turkey, but being forbidden by the Holy Spirit to preach there. They plan to go east to provinces bordering the south coast of the Black Sea, but again the Holy Spirit forbids this. So they continue westward and arrive at Troas. Then, in a night vision, a man of Macedonia pleads with Paul: "Come over to Macedonia and help us", which meant his going west not east.

As a result of the Lord's guiding through this passage, I 'looked westward' – and there was the Mercy Ship m/v *Anastasis* in Jamaica. I phoned my daughter, who was serving onboard at the time, to say that I was coming. She replied, "No, mummy, it's not a time to visit. We are on a medical mission."

A few days later, I received an airmail letter from her, saying that the leader of the YWAM Jamaica centre had come aboard and sent greetings to me, saying, "Tell her to come over and help us." Needing no further confirmation, I booked my ticket and went.

Island in the sun

Jamaica is one of the larger islands in the Caribbean. It has lush vegetation, wonderful fruit, beautiful waterfalls, and dazzling white beaches. It is therefore an international tourist attraction. Sadly, in contrast to the island's very few rich, most Jamaican people live in poverty. Family structure is collapsing, as over 85 per cent of the children are born out of wedlock (1989 figures).

In the summer of 1988, Hurricane *Gilbert* swept through the island, destroying property and leaving many thousands homeless. The economy was severely affected, as bananas and other crops had been flattened. That's why the *Anastasis* made several trips to the island, bringing relief of every kind. Hundreds were being touched by God's love. It was a wonderful springboard for the gospel.

On my arrival in Jamaica, Mercy Ships staff gave me a visitor's badge, and several well-meaning people wished me "a good holiday". I smiled and waited. Two days later, there was my daughter apologising to me because she was going ashore to do registration for the dental team, which needed assistance. Being a woman of God, it only took her seconds to say, "Would you like to come and help?" It took me even fewer seconds to reply, "Yes."

After two hectic days, it was Wednesday 15 June 1988 – my 68th birthday. The frantic crowds had eased off, so the dental leader said, "Florence, would you like to show the *Jesus* video to the people waiting for their appointments?" I said, "Yes, but what about all those queuing hopefully outside? Can I speak to them?"

She said, "Okay," so I went outside and shouted, "Who has pain?" Every hand went up. I then said, "Where will your pain be if you die tonight?" Silence! I explained that we have body, soul and spirit and that when we die, pain is gone, but according to Jesus our spirits will be either with God forever or lost forever in the place where there will be gnashing of teeth. I followed that with what it means to follow Jesus.

When I asked for a response with commitment to Jesus, 18 people stepped forward. I thanked God for a wonderful birthday present, and the dentists were thrilled. It seems that it had not occurred to them that people could be saved daily while the clinic was running. The following week was pure joy for me as many others prayed for salvation and a changed life.

From that time on, the Mercy Ships leader and her successor sent me faxes of invitation, saying which country they were in and which dates would be best for me to come. This led to many visits to different nations, the Lord providing finance through whomsoever He would and giving me the strength and health that I needed.

An outreach with real teeth

It was my privilege to be the full-time evangelist with the Mandeville Jamaica Dental Team in January-March 1989. We were at 3,000 feet and only had cold water for showers – ugh! It rained frequently, staining shoes, legs, and clothes with red mud, because of the bauxite in the soil. The stains were hard to remove, especially with cold water. The drinking water was generally unsafe (as is often the case in such nations), as were many foods, especially milk products. All fruit had to be washed in bleach. Sleeping accommodation proved that you could get a pint out of a half-pint pot!

That was the downside. This outreach was wonderful, however, as the Lord blessed every day with people coming to salvation, physical healings and changed lives. Here are a few stories.

Clifton was a gentle Rastafarian who was entranced to hear about 'my' Jesus who was neither black nor white, and who said,

"those who have seen Me, have seen the Father".

Clifton gave his life to Jesus.

Peter was a 20 year old who came to the clinic on the last day with no appointment. The dentists took an X-ray and removed a tooth with an unseen abscess. I pointed out that God had a second divine appointment to open up his heart and expose the decay there. When asked, "Who do you say Jesus is?" he replied "God." Shades of another man called Peter! Thank God this one gave his heart to the Lord.

Paulette saw a sign in the sky, and told her mother, who said, "God is calling you." The next day she came to the clinic and heard me say, "Today, when you hear His voice, don't harden your heart." She wept copiously and gladly gave her heart to Jesus. She had been with the same man for nine years with no children and knew that now it was marriage or the end of that relationship. Wonder of wonders! Two school friends with her, on hearing her and seeing her radiance, were also "born again".

During the eighth week, instead of travelling back to the *Anastasis* for some rest and relaxation, I accepted an invitation to stay with a Jamaican lady called Caroldine. Although a Christian only 18 months, she was totally devoted to bringing in God's kingdom. She had established prayer rooms in several towns across Jamaica, which were maintained by the fruit of her labours in the insurance business.

On Sunday 12 March, accompanied by a pastor and his wife, we went to take devotions for the 'troublesome' girl boarders at Caroldine's daughter's school. Two hours later, all 16 girls were committed to a changed lifestyle. The following Wednesday the pastor had booked a 'teaching' session, but the Lord bade me return for the six girls who had been absent the previous weekend. They were also 'born again' and all were filled with the Spirit. Everyone abounded with joy, including the matron.

In-between, and following those visits, we travelled daily to Black River and Kingston via Spanish Town. There, a young man just out of prison was waiting for prayer with his mother and sister. When asked how old he was, he said "59"! Having addressed bondages (to drugs, alcohol, and sex), he said that he wanted to know Jesus. Clearly and lucidly he repented, received cleansing by the blood of Jesus, and asked Him to be his Lord. He was actually 23 years old.

"The kingdom of God is not a matter of talk but of power." (1 Cor 4:20)

Our time in Jamaica was blessed as the Lord saved, healed, and delivered through whatever channels were available. No wonder that in November 1989 Satan tried to kill my Jamaican sister Caroldine and her daughter, Isaac the bridegroom, and myself as we were driving to the wedding rehearsal and the trying-on of wedding outfits.

The road twisted and turned constantly. Suddenly Isaac and I simultaneously and spontaneously broke into tongues. An instant later, the wheel was wrenched from Isaac's hands as we went round a bend, and we went straight into the rock-face. Any vehicle coming in the opposite direction would have hit us, as we were skewed across the road.

Having examined the damage, and straightened up a wing which was touching a tyre, Isaac pulled away from the rock-face and we limped on.

Soon we caught up with a huge lorry going so slowly that we had to pass it. Isaac accelerated, but when we were level with the lorry and facing oncoming traffic, the tyre blew. We had to draw back. We were all shaken but praised God all the way to our destination. On arrival, our car was taken to a repair shop, where the mechanics said that it was a total write-off and that they didn't see how we could have driven it! We didn't, God did! How I praised God for all that He did.

Jamaica provided one other encouraging story. While there I met a Malay Indian whom my pioneer team of five (mentioned in Chapter 1) had met and prayed for in Malaysia, in August 1981. He told me that he has been serving the Lord ever since and had studied on several YWAM schools, been on two FEET teams and worked as an itinerant evangelist. Here he was leading an SOE team from Canada. All his Hindu family were now Christian. Who knows what God is doing as we meet and pray for or with people? Isn't that thought exciting?

Mercy Ships

Mercy Ships serves in developing countries in many ways. Construction teams build houses and schools and repair roofs. Medical clinics go into villages to give free medical care. Surgeries are held onboard: sight is given when congenital cataracts are removed and crossed eyes are straightened. One patient who was a schoolteacher said, "Now my students will know who I'm looking at." Cleft lips and palates are repaired, huge tumours removed, horrific burns treated, teeth cared for. Agricultural teams sow and instruct. Healthcare teams teach women how to help themselves and their families, and dental hygienists teach how to care for your teeth. What a wonderful ministry! Particularly as in lots of developing nations one dentist or doctor will serve many thousands of people, so many cannot get help even if they can pay for it.

No-one working for Mercy Ships receives a salary – not even the captain. In fact they pay to serve. I counted it a privilege to be with them.

Chapter 14

Mercy Ship Outreach to The Dominican Republic (1989)

Hispaniola: just another idyllic island in the Caribbean? Actually, it is an island split in two: one-third is Haiti, the poorest country in the Western hemisphere, and two-thirds is the Dominican Republic (DR). The DR is still suffering after the 33-year reign of Dictator Tuijillo. Under his regime of terror, many disappeared, with no questions asked and no action taken. This left the people seeking answers to life, and the majority in dire poverty. One Christian Dominican man encouraged the Mercy Ship leaders to send a ship with the two-handed gospel! They did, in the summer of 1989.

When I prayed, the Lord said, "Shake the trees and gather the fruit now. Ripe fruit rots when it is left on the ground." So I went for six weeks. What a harvest! The first month was spent in the towns of Barahona, where the *Anastasis* was berthed, and Tomayo. I filled in more than a thousand cards of commitment. Here are some of the stories behind those cards.

Ludia was a 23-year-old widow left with several children to raise. She was so poor that the people from her village paid for the 13-hour bus trip to get her to the ship. She was full of fear as she waited in the ward for her small son's recovery from a cleft lip and palate operation. The boy also had club hands and feet, so had to be carried everywhere.

After hearing the gospel, she received Jesus as her Saviour. The Lord showed me that I was to take her on my lap, with the boy on hers. He was on a drip, and breathing heavily from a bronchial complication. Then God told me to say to her, "Weep, woman." She did. Other words of comfort followed such as, "You are safe and secure with Me today and always – you are My child and I love you with an everlasting love." Then I had to sing to her a song about His love and peace. She slept in my arms like a baby.

After 30 minutes my arms and legs were numb. She awoke, I prayed for the boy's speedy physical recovery and left. Some days later, the examining doctor said that the boy's mouth had miraculously healed. Ludia went home wreathed in smiles, waving until out of sight. She was still a poor widow and her son still had club hands and feet, but now Jesus was in her heart, and it was as if someone had turned a light on inside her. The Lord is a life-changer!

Julio, aged 65 years, did not get help on the ship's first visit, though he did feel great love. He returned, heard the Good News, repented with tears, and, when prayed for, shook and jumped up and down. When asked if he had a problem, he said, "No, it is God's power on me, I feel as though I could fly." Isn't the Lord good? He brings such a transformation to individuals.

Lidia immediately demanded prayer for her son. Her face was sullen, but when she heard the gospel and said, "Yes," the Lord told me to give her a swing! Recruiting a young man, we obeyed. Lidia laughed and laughed, which continued until she left some days later, infecting parents and relatives of patients with sheer joy. Simple acts can bring deep healing to those deprived of a normal childhood and love.

One day at the Tomayo clinic, a group of 40 new Christians came for medical help. They all lived in one village called Laskejas. As they had some time to wait, I started to speak to them. Suddenly I found myself cutting them off from witchcraft, generational sin, and sickness. I marched round them, breaking curses and separating them from their forebears. Then I spoke on healing and prayed for it to flow. Everyone responded to the call to follow Jesus! Several declared themselves healed before seeing the doctor.

Later, they all went home to their village, but not before I challenged one 18-year-old to remove all idols from his home and burn them. A week later, the village pastor arrived and invited me to go back with him and see what was happening. I took two or three others with me, plus a translator. On arrival, the place looked deserted. It was in fact a desolate dust bowl.

We headed for the church, and I could hardly believe my eyes. It was packed with village residents all praising God. It seemed that the young man had invited the whole village to burn occult symbols, books, and jewellery, and as they praised God around the blaze, people had been healed of long-term illnesses and one of mental problems. The people prayed for rain and had plans to plant and sow crops, believing that, as God was with them, they would succeed. They had no clean water, no electricity, no work and previously no hope. Now they had hope. Praise God.

We visited the Army Vocational boys' school. There were 180 residents, typical teens who were playing it tough. I was given permission to speak, and 150 boys came. I quote from a subsequent letter: "When you spoke, they fell silent and were totally riveted on your words. Afterwards they flocked to you like babies." I know that a 108 out of the 150 prayed to follow Jesus.

Those who had come with me and witnessed what God had done wanted to put it on video, which meant a "repeat" performance. Doubting that it could be done, I asked if I could return, and was given permission. Now I had told these boys that God answered prayers if they were reasonable. Well, we returned and, to my amazement, there were even more than on the previous visit. I asked for testimonies, and these lads came forward with stories of answered prayer. One had needed shoes – and they appeared outside his door. Another required money for books, and it came. And so on. After that, still more responded to the gospel message.

We were in their dining room. I climbed up on a table and rebuked Satan, reminding him that he was defeated at Calvary and now these young men belonged to Jesus. I encouraged them to draw near to God and resist the devil (James 4:7), all in the powerful name of Jesus. My translator, at that time a Canadian policeman, carried me to our vehicle. When I asked why, he said I was a princess and deserved royal treatment.

Dignara, aged 18 years, came to the *Anastasis* hoping that the orthopaedic surgeon could help her congenital scoliosis condition. They sent her to me for prayer. I asked her if she was a believer, and she said that she attended the Mormon Church. That day she heard the true gospel and received Jesus as her Saviour.

I then asked her to sit on a chair, take off her shoes, and lift her feet, which revealed one leg shorter than the other by at least an inch. Watched by my Dominican translator, as I prayed, the shorter leg grew immediately to the same length as the longer leg. The Lord had brought her to the ship to be saved and healed in 23 minutes. The translator told everyone in sight, resigned her job, signed on as crew, and continued serving for several years.

Sunilda came with two children and no husband to the dental clinic and, on hearing the Word, asked Jesus into her heart. Shortly afterwards,

I saw the dentist praying with her for her sick mother and, later still, a nurse who said, "Florence, this is the lady who wrote me a letter asking if we could give her a new roof to her home, as the rain comes in."

I asked Sunilda what was wrong with her mother. She said, "She has had six abortions and her stomach is hanging out." A visit revealed that her home was really terrible, her father going blind, and her mother a woman in advanced stages of malnutrition. All seemed hopeless until we learned that her parents had become Christians two months previously, and then some powerful prayers went up for shelter, food, and clothes.

The construction team had a full programme and all looked hopeless, but God, who does the impossible, caused time and materials to be multiplied, so that in two days all these prayers were answered. The gospel was preached too, and 32 people were saved in that one village, which, I believe, will never be the same again. Most were unable to read, so the pastor received a Bible in Spanish on tape, for his congregation to hear the Word.

A beautiful 22-year-old girl came to the Tomayo medical clinic, elegantly dressed yet on crutches as she had a missing foot. I was called in, as there was spiritual darkness evident on her beautiful face. Questioning revealed that her foot had been accidentally severed by her stepfather when she was two years old. She was encouraged to release forgiveness toward God and man, and on hearing of the suffering of Jesus, she wept and received Him into her heart. The next day, as we recommended, she went to the ship and got the very last lower-leg prosthesis. She was able to walk away, a beautiful, joyous young lady.

On my first visit, I left Barahona to serve for two weeks with the m/v *Good Samaritan*, a smaller Mercy Ship docked in Puerto Viejo. The dental clinic was working here, alongside the hosting medical clinic. On day one, the native male worker received Jesus; on day two, the cleaner; and on day three, the doctor in charge. His lady assistant was already the Lord's, so praise God, there was totally Christian staff to work with and leave behind.

I had angelic help in that clinic. Holding a huge silver bowl filled with toothbrushes to give to the children, I entered the room. Immediately, I was being pushed and shoved by many children: a toothbrush is a real treasure to those who have never possessed one. It was scary, so I called, "Help, Lord!" Suddenly, the children were making way for a huge black man. He towered over me and must have looked like a giant to the kids. He took the bowl and held it above his head. Silence reigned. He lowered the bowl to my level, and I handed out all the toothbrushes in perfect peace. When the bowl was empty, he disappeared. That man was not someone I had seen before, nor saw again throughout my two weeks in the clinic. Thank you, Lord, for that angelic visitation and the work of your angelic host!

Chapter 15

Mercy Ship Outreach to Togo, West Africa (1991)

*"And as you preach… heal the sick, raise the
dead, cleanse the lepers, cast out demons,
freely you have received, freely give"*
Matt. 10 7,8

Where in the world is Togo?

I t is on the West coast of Africa, bordered by Benin to the north, It
is long and narrow, roughtly 500km in length and 100km in width.
Up-country are game parks with wildlife, but in the south are
wonderful beaches, where teams of fishermen can be seen hauling in
huge nets to rhythmic singing. Sadly their catch, unlike their nets, is
small. Most of the people I found there were animists, and in 1991 life
expectancy was around 50 for both male and female. French is the
official language, but there are also several tribal languages.

The *Anastasis* docked in Lome, the capital. I showed the *Jesus* film in
the dental clinic every day, preaching frequently from the teachings of
Jesus. Many came to the Kingdom.

Surgeons operated on cleft lip and palate, huge tumours and burns,
giving many a new quality of lie in this world, whilst demonstrating
the love of God. In Togo at that time, a new baby born with a clift lip
or palate was considered to be demonised. The witch doctors
performed a special ceremony that consisted of placing the baby in a
wooden box and burying the infant alive.

One father, who was a Christian, knew that the ceremony was
wrong. When his daughter was born with a cleft palate, he named her
Piranem, which means "we value you" – and he refused to give her up
to the witch-doctors. The villagers forced him to leave. Nine years later,
a van came to his new home town of Kara in the north, full of medical

people. Piranem was accepted for surgery – and without cost. This Christian family returned to the village that had driven them out and were a wonderful testimony that an operation could restore birth damage.

Jesus came to take dominion over sin, sickness, demons, nature and death itself. Here are some more stories to show that He is the same yesterday, today and forever.

Sin

791 were saved as they repented of sin, and gave their lives to Jesus in the Dental Clinic.

Sickness

Sikani Lawson, a beautiful Togolese lady responded to the Gospel early in the outreach. She had lost a baby four months previously. She repented of her anger and bitterness, and was thrilled to hear that her little one would be in heaven. However she returned, complaining of heart, stomach and leg pain. We prayed in Jesus' Name. She received the Holy Spirit with singing and dancing, and went on her way rejoicing. She returned on our last day to say "Thank you" – absolutely radiant, and declaring that she was free from all pain.

Demons

Togo was 70% animist, and voodoo abounded. Many adults, children and babies were wearing fetishes to ward off evil spirits. Sadly this practice opens the door to demonic forces. Happily we have the victory in the Name of Jesus. Many who heard the Gospel allowed fetishes to be cut off from wrists, ankles and waists – and gave them to me to be destroyed, having accepted Jesus as *"Mahout"* (God).

Nature

One day, as the dental team stopped for lunch, I saw huge eyes looking through the shutters. I asked if anyone was willing to give up one of their two huge sandwiches and/or their apple. Some responded. I quartered the eight sandwiches and sliced the four apples and asked my friend Suzette, the dental team leader, to go to the waiting room where children were watching the *Jesus* video, to count them. She returned saying that there were at least fifty. We prayed that there would be enough with none left over – and it was so. Not one left out – and none left over. Praise the Lord! He is still the God of miracles, big and small.

Death

I was called to the ward one evening to pray for an eight-year-old boy with a huge tumour on his face, which the doctor said would kill him very soon. **Death** was rebuked, the boy was cut off from curses of all kinds and various demonic spirits were addressed, as the Holy Spirit revealed. The cancer was commanded to wither and die. Then we praised the Lord.

Before leaving the ship, I asked the doctor why nothing could be done for the boy. He explained that this kind of tumour came from a virus peculiar to that area, which was fast growing and inoperable. He also said that the boy had received chemotherapy at the Lome hospital, that the tumour was already smaller, and that the treatment was expected to be successful. Who minds how or why, as long as a boy lives, and death is defeated in Jesus' mighty Name!

Miracle

One day I felt led to go with the agricultural team. Two nurses came along to set up a minor treatment clinic in the back of the van. One of the nurses asked if I would pray for a "poor soul" whom she had met on a previous visit. The woman came out of her hut, bent like a letter Z. She said that she had not stood upright for five years. Examination revealed a huge hernia in her groin and a tumour under her arm. Having no common language, a man came along who had enough words to explain repentance and salvation. She gave her heart to Jesus. Satan's bondage was broken, with all curses. The Lord told me to take her hands and say, "Woman! Rise in the Name of Jesus!" And she did. Both nurses walked away.

Once upright, the Spirit told me to hold her, love her and sing to her. She was thin and frail, but I felt strength pouring into her body. I raised her hands in praise to Jesus, saying "Hallelujah!". She said the same. After a while, I called a nurse over and, holding our arms, she walked the length of the village, where everyone knew her. We returned and I suggested she rested. She entered her hut, but came out again to say "Thank you" in French. Just like the leper in the Bible.

At 1pm *South Sea Waves* came to perform dance and song. After a while along came 'Solly', arms in the air, singing "Hallelujah!" When the agricultural team leader saw her, he asked the story, but before he could tell it, 'Solly' took the microphone and told the whole assembled village that she had begun the day wracked with pain, but that Jesus had healed her. We had the translation of what she had said from the *South Sea Waves* translator – and he asked if he could join my organisation!

Next day, people were heading for the village. One blind man, picked up on the road the next morning, said, "God is moving there." On the following Sunday, over three hundred attended the service, including 'Solly'.

The wonderful end to this story is that a construction team were already there building a school which of course, in God's marvellous plan, became their church. A team returned to the village from the *Anastasis*, for a mass baptism. The Lord built his church in Djegbakodji for His glory

Chapter 16

Mercy Ship Outreach
in Poland and Baltic States
(1991-95)

Estonia and Poland (1991)

*"Call upon me in the day of
trouble; I will deliver you, and you
will honour me."* Ps 50:15

Tallinn, Estonia, Monday 19 August 1991: we awoke on the
Mercy Ship *Anastasis* to find ourselves blockaded by three
Russian warships and forbidden to go ashore. History was in the
making, and we were in the thick of it. Communist hardliners had
staged their bid to topple President Gorbachev and seize control of the
Kremlin.

The crew were called to pray, but not many were free to respond. We
prayed that the KGB would split and that the 'coup' would fail. The
Lord showed us from Judges chapter 7 that with a few we could win,
and from 2 Chronicles 20:17 that we were to stand still and see Him
do it. So we sang and praised the Lord for the victory.

The next day we heard that the KGB had split and the coup had
failed. A special few were escorted ashore to collect our much-needed
dental chairs and evangelistic equipment. We were then free to sail
away, but sadly without saying goodbye to our newfound Estonian
friends and family in Christ. Our visit had been cut short, but even so,
seeds had been sown – the gospel was preached with healing and
deliverance, believers were encouraged, and the Lord again saved those
who were His. What a loving, wonderful God we serve!

Just before this episode, the *Anastasis* had docked in Gdansk, Poland,
for a week. The onboard team of volunteers from several Western

countries served the Polish people with expert dental care, or whatever blessings the Lord would channel through them.

I was asked to preach on the docks. No-one responded to my first altar-call, at which – it was reported – I cried, "Are you crazy? We are talking about your eternal home." Pointing to the ship, I continued. "If they invited you to sail on her but said that it could sink like the *Titanic*, would you not be thinking about whether it would be heaven or hell for you forever? You do not know whether you have another day on earth, so consider Jesus your only hope."

Then many responded, followed by hours of prayer. The Lord reaped those who were His, healed whom He would, and was a Wonderful Counsellor to others.

Lithuania (1993)

Freedom was a fairly new concept for Lithuanians when the *Anastasis* docked in Klaipeda, Lithuania, in the summer of 1993. A beautiful land of lakes and forests inhabited by a delightful but hurting people, here was another Baltic nation that had been dominated by external forces for generations, and been left with a devastating shortage of everything.

Tears flowed as seven trailers of medical and dental supplies arrived, together with a volunteer dental team from various nations, to offer much-needed dental care for three weeks.

During clinic hours, the *Jesus* film was shown and, after the video was stopped at various key teachings of Jesus, the gospel was preached several times daily. One of teachings was when Jesus quoted from Isaiah in Luke 4:18-19:

"The Spirit of the Lord is on me, because he has
anointed me to preach good news to the poor.
He has sent me to proclaim freedom for the prisoners
and recovery of sight for the blind, to release the
oppressed, to proclaim the year of the Lord's favour,"

and sent His followers out to do likewise
(Matt 10:1; Luke 9:1-2).

With reminders such as that, when a young man who said he was a Satanist asked me for prayer, I took him into another room to pray for deliverance. This took a while and was noisy, causing some to ask, "What is going on?" When you fulfil the Lord's commands, it is often misunderstood, even by Christians.

However, we received much appreciation. Over 10,000 heard the gospel, and, according to a report, 1,300 professed a first-time commitment to Jesus. The mayor of Klaipeda stated, "We are thankful for the material help, but more important for our nation is the spiritual help." And he did not profess to being a Christian! A reporter said of the visit, "We have listened to your message of love and you have demonstrated it – sacrificing your lives for others. You have shown us how to love, which is difficult for us after years of fear and hatred."

Here are some examples of how the team showed the love of Jesus to the people.

Mr and Mrs Lipinskas, who were in their 50s, were on their way to the fourth floor of the dental clinic, hoping for dentures, as he was toothless. The gospel was being preached. They turned around and walked down the stairs to listen. Despite hearing only half of the message, they both received Jesus, she with tears, he with much joy. They had a divine appointment and went home rejoicing. Better to be toothless and saved for eternity than to have lovely false teeth and be lost forever!

Rema brought her son to the clinic. He had stuttered since being attacked by bigger boys and refused to open his mouth to receive treatment. Both his mother and grandmother responded to the gospel. I took them aside and said I believed a spirit of fear had entered the boy. They asked me to pray. After telling a demonic spirit to go, in the power and authority of Jesus, it went with a screech. The boy went into the clinic and allowed the dentist to both look and work on his teeth! All three came to the Bible study and, after two hours of truths from the Word, left with shining faces. God was glorified through something that was meant for evil.

Jurgita, a 19-year-old who was translating for a tour guide, was raised a Catholic, though she had been unable to attend church as it was forbidden under communism. Her schoolteachers taught that God did not exist; the Russian cosmonauts returned to earth and said, "He is not up there." Children mocked if she asked a question. Then the ship came. Jurgita plied us with questions, avid to hear. When she saw the *Jesus* video she joyfully responded and communicated the gospel immediately with boldness to everyone she met. She and others like her are Lithuania's hope, as they speak truth with love and power.

Latvia (1995)

Strands of gold – "The threads of four unique lives were woven together to minister health and hope to the people of Latvia."

As I looked out from the side of the *Anastasis*, I could feel its dark presence. Even though it had been abandoned a few years before, the deserted Russian watchtower overlooking the port of Vilnius was still a grim reminder of terrible times. As was the barbed wire that still festooned the length of the beach. The struggle of the Latvian people's tumultuous history had left a legacy of grief, despair, and fear. These lovely people were still reeling from 70 years of communism.

It was the summer of 1995 in Vilnius, and I was one of four strands: Elaine (30), from the Isle of Wight in England, sung songs in Latvian; Wendy (51), from the UK, told Bible stories with much passion; Kay (57), from the USA, taught dental health, using puppets and humour; and finally myself, Florence, a 75-year-old evangelist from the UK, preached and gave testimony to a God who heals. The four of us had arrived in Latvia on the *Anastasis* as part of the dental clinic for children, some of whom came onboard accompanied by adults.

Here are a few stories from our time in Latvia, on what proved to be my last mission with the *Anastasis*.

One woman, who had asked for prayer before one of our meetings, declared herself saved and healed after hearing that unforgiveness makes us sick and that the Bible says "when you stand praying, forgive or your Father will not forgive you". There were tears as children and adults gave their lives to Jesus.

One day, two platoons of soldiers came onboard to see the ship and hear the Good News. I was asked to preach. Some of the officers responded, after which some of the privates raised their hands. Fear of man is a snare; man can only kill the body – God can kill body and soul (Matt 10:28).

I shared a cabin with a 76-year-old Latvian lady married to an American. We were given freedom to minister wherever the Spirit led. At a nursing home in the town of Ventspils, some of the old folk comprehended the love of God as the Scriptures were preached. Some wept with repentance and joy, feeling safe at last.

In a children's orphanage, the young ones loved the puppets and dramas, and all but one of the teenagers gave their lives to the Lord. An outreach team from Texas, USA, performed dramas and songs on the dock every day. They asked me to preach to the many waiting to tour the ship. There was a good response. Our cabin became so full of flowers we could hardly move.

Sometimes, Anna and I were onboard to speak with the visitors at the end of their tour. We gave them a Bible study on the basic scriptures, reinforcing the gospel. On one occasion we were laughing so hard, I couldn't speak. I finally said, "We have 151 years between us that say 'We know where we are going, no matter what is happening in the world.' We will laugh our way to heaven and so can you." People responded, some prayed for salvation, and a spirit of joy took over.

On our last evening, I had escaped to a friend's cabin to rest after six hours of praying over a pastor, his family, and his church – the need for such a long time of prayer being because the pastor had first sought witchcraft for healing rather than God.

Another pastor – very tall, very thin, with eyes like burning coals – came to the ship with an English-speaking pastor, asking for me. Would I go back with them, he asked?

I wanted to say "No," but they told me that the whole church was waiting for me, 50 miles away in Ugali. "It is not possible," I said, "all the vehicles are onboard, and all crew must return by 9pm." They said, "We will drive you there and back." For them, that meant driving 50 miles, four times, in a land where cars were scarce and petrol scarcer. Such was the imperative, I went.

The Lord quickened Matt 5:1-12 to me, so, on arrival, I spoke on "Beautiful attitudes". There was much repentance, with tears. I then prayed for the women who had come out to receive the Holy Spirit. Each one fell down laughing, crying, or as dead. The men followed, including both pastors! I said, "What now, Lord?" He said to wait. Fifteen minutes later, the English-speaking pastor moved, so I said that I must go. He roused the other pastor. We walked out between the bodies, and arrived back just in time for curfew.

Chapter 17

First Outreach in Albania with YWAM (1992)

Dilapidated buildings in need of repair and paint. Windows that were boarded up or missing panes of glass. Shops with almost nothing to sell. Rubbish everywhere. No newspapers, magazines, books, maps, or even toilet paper. Welcome to Albania one year after the fall of communism – and specifically the town of Shkoder in the north of the country.

I had been invited in May 1992 to join a team from the *Anastasis* DTS in Shkoder. The town's streets were packed with people, yet this was actually a sad sight. For the multitudes were unemployed men, still wearing donated and outdated Western bell-bottomed trousers, smoking, and playing cards. Bicycles were everywhere. There was no police control. People were clamouring for bread, or for whatever else was being delivered that day. Here and there were street vendors, some selling a few chocolate bars or sweets, others with homemade cakes, but few passers-by had money to spend. Shkoder was one massive builder's yard.

Here were these delightful people, living in what should have been a beautiful land of lakes, mountains, and rivers, but was instead so ugly and barren, having lain uncultivated for many years. Enver Hoxha, the communist ruler of Albania, had declared the country to be Europe's first atheistic state. All places of worship had been closed, all holy books destroyed. Consequently, when communism fell in 1991 there was nothing to take its place.

Institutional reform

Our team of 16, from 11 nations and including one surgeon, one doctor, and five nurses, found ourselves going to many people from institutions. We visited all kinds of establishments – prisons, orphanages, children's homes, toddler's homes, and homes for people suffering from dystrophy. Wherever we went, we left clothes, crayons, and books.

The greatest joy was at a "deficiency hospital", where the patients were afraid of us at first, but soon received God's love, joy, and laughter through the team. We went there three times. We loved them, and they loved us. One room contained those patients who constantly hit their heads against the walls. A young Canadian and I sat among them and prayed. As we did so, peace and calm descended on them, and their tremendous shaking ceased. How people in this kind of situation need those who will even just go and pray with them.

We also visited political prisoners who were still in prison to assess their medical or material needs. Some of their stories were dreadfully sad. For instance, three brothers that I met had between them spent 102 years in prison because their sister had escaped to Yugoslavia.

Before leaving England, I had cried out to God to use me, and He had answered by pairing me with a 19-year-old Swiss girl and giving us the home of a family of four professors to stay in for the duration of the outreach. Consequently, we had wide access to students in the university, in high and middle schools, and in a college of music. We saw much fruit, and were able to hold a daily Bible study as well as our daily team meetings in the university.

Open doors

Our host family was very talented, yet their joint income was a mere US$50 a month. This led inevitably to much trading on the black market. But family ties are strong in Albania: the 26 and 23-year-old daughters of our host did the cleaning and washing every Saturday, so that on the following Monday everyone could go to work wearing the same clothes. I saw their mother wear nothing but the same clean outfit the whole time we were there. Elie, her daughter and my translator, did the same. Every evening from 6.30-9pm, it was time to visit friends and family, when coffee and a sweet were offered, a tradition arising from the 500 years of Turkish rule which ended in 1904.

On Sundays, we all went for walks, because there was really nothing else to do. We went with our host family to Shkoder Castle. It was so peaceful there, with no portable sound systems blaring out music and no vehicles. On our second Sunday the family took us to a beautiful lake. But this visit was a sad one, as it was a time when they remembered those who had died trying to swim for nine hours to freedom in Yugoslavia. Some had been shot by the border guards.

At one point I was taken to see Enver Hoxha's former residence. It had 17 rooms, all with TV and fridge, and a fleet of vehicles. Hoxha was universally hated by Albanians, who believed that Paradise began outside their borders. When I told them that they must forgive Hoxha, they shouted "Never!" I pointed out that they had had 45 years under one kind of evil, but the West, during that same period, had opened its doors to many other kinds of evil. But at that time, I found it impossible to convince the Albanians. They thought that there was nothing more wonderful than to escape. Those who did escape (mainly into Greece) found themselves unemployed, sleeping on the streets, and harassed by the police, who sent them back to Albania.

I told them that, when paper returned to Albania, pornography would come with it, leading to a breakdown in this wonderful Albanian family life. On my second visit to Shkoder in 1993, I was shocked and saddened to see broadsheet newspapers spread out on the pavement, where unemployed men were gazing at their leisure at full-page pictures of nude girls. Yes, it happened!

So ended my first visit to Albania, totally filled with wonderful exciting things, hundreds and hundreds of children hearing about Jesus Christ for the first time; sitting on the grass with university students, telling them that they were not Muslims, nor were they Catholics, nor were they Orthodox because they had had no possibility of following their beliefs – so they were ready to listen after I had told them that, and why not.

Chapter 18

To Albania again to join a team, but with no address

On a later visit – and I have put this story in here to immediately follow the previous chapter – to Albania and Tirana the capital, I found myself on a plane – on the way to join a team – without a name or an address to go to – surely rather a problem? Standing outside the airport, expecting to be met, but recognising no-one, I announced, "My name is Florence Robertson. Is anybody waiting for me?" No response. Taxi drivers and boys begging assailed me constantly.

One hour later, I agreed by signs to pay 70 dollars to a very persistent taxi driver to take me to Korce. I knew from my instructions that Korce was five hours drive over three mountain passes, and four in the vehicle must pay 25 dollars each to be driven there.

The man took me to a beautiful new white vehicle with royal blue velvet seats in this land where, at that time, there were only rusty battered cars. Another man was at the wheel, and off we went, but after seeing the glory of a setting sun over the first Pass, I fell asleep.

They awakened me, saying "Korce!" A vista of many lights around a mountain met my gaze, and I realized that Korce was a very well-spread-out huge city. Now came the tricky part. I had no name, address or a phone number. This fact perplexed my escort. Shrugging their shoulders, though, and without asking for money, they took me into the main hotel, where the manager said that someone was coming who could speak English.

He came, but when I said that I had no name or address, he left, also shrugging his shoulders. By God's grace, a boy was listening and said something – at which everyone piled into the taxi, including the hotel manager.

When it stopped, they knocked at the door. Someone replied, and they took off again. This second young boy had said something and they were all going, minus the hotel manager.

At the second stop in this city of some 70,000 inhabitants, I asked "Doctor? Medicine? Ameya Carmo?" After a pause, the lady at the door said, "Doctor S". I flew past her, ran into the house – and there was my team! Their mouths dropped open and the leader said, "How can you possibly have got here?" I replied, "God!"

My team thought that I had gone home; my husband thought that I was with the team, and at that time people were being killed for a case of clothes, not to mention money, cameras and other valuables that foreign visitors would normally carry. Who were those two men? I had so many wonderful examples of God's help and assistance.

Now back to 1993…

Chapter 19

Outreach in Guinea with Mercy Ships (1993)

A new year and a new challenge in a new region! In January 1993, I was asked if I could join as co-leader of an *Anastasis* DTS outreach team, which was leaving at the end of the month for Guinea, West Africa. After a quick trip home from Sierra Leone where I had been preaching and teaching (some of the preaching being on the *Anastasis* when it was in Freetown) to re-equip and acquire a visa, I too was off to Guinea.

What a blessed time! Tom Moore, a pastor, had arranged the eight-week trip. He met me and took me by pick-up truck for many hours from Conakry to the bauxite-mining town of Kamsar in the north, where I joined the outreach team of seven. Tom brought the *Jesus* film with him, which we showed every night from the back of our pick-up truck, and which Tom and I used as the basis for our preaching in either the local tribal language Susu (Tom) or French (me). We toured the "bush" daily, announcing the film by megaphone, as well as holding open-air meetings in the town.

Unfortunately, we were there during the month of Ramadan, so no-one appeared before 8.30pm (each day, from dusk till then, they were eating their fast-breaking meal). What with the film being two hours long and the frequent breakdowns of the projector, we were often there until 1am. But it was worth it. Tom reckoned that as many as 2,000 were present each evening.

The icing on the cake appeared later in a newsletter that Tom sent out. As he wrote: "I returned to Guinea in December 1994 for two weeks to visit the Christians and pastors, and to see how the work was going on with no direct missionary involvement."

Tom then mentioned good reports from four towns, including Kamsar. There had been joint services with 12 baptisms. Also, there had been an incident where a family member had poisoned one of the pastors, as he was the eldest son of a strong Muslim family. Yet, through prayer, after three days of vomiting, he recovered.

Tom continued: "Those of you who did spiritual groundwork in Kamsar should know that a beautiful church has been built for Pastor Joseph and his family. Many continue to come to the Lord, and great things are happening there. The fruit is evident and is the direct result of your faithful labour there."

Two small groups of DTS students, spending eight weeks in Guinea, West Africa – and the effects are still there. Seeds bear fruit. In the Bible, the apostle Paul says:

> **"I planted the seed, Apollos watered it,
> but God made it grow."**
>
> (1 Cor 3:6)

Glory to God! He did.

Chapter 20

Outreach in Norway with King's Kids (1994)

"Woe is me if I do not preach the gospel!"
1 Cor 9:16

I knew I had to be there, so I just went. It was February 1994, and the Winter Olympics were being held in Lillehammer, Norway. The leader of the YWAM centre surely heard from God when he placed me as the evangelist with a team from King's Kids Norway. These young people, handpicked from cities across Norway, had been meeting once a month for some time. They told me that they had been praying for a grandmother but not, I suspect, one like me!

When we arrived, the Lord gave me a picture. It was of fairyland, pure white everywhere. Then He told me to get a shovel and dig. I did, in the Spirit, and saw dry, barren earth producing nothing. State religions in several European countries were not growing. Many Norwegians, I am told, are returning to Nordic or Greek mythology. How sad.

Cold war

The Lord had also given me 1 Corinthians 16:9, which promises a *'great door'* open for ministry but warns of *'many who oppose'*. We certainly saw this verse in action. For instance, one day, our 50-seater bus went into a ditch of deep snow, but a tractor appeared out of nowhere and the driver towed us out. On another occasion, air entered the diesel fuel of our bus and we broke down. Here we were in another desolate place, yet an empty "official" bus came along and took us to our ministry destination. In yet another episode, the engine went "kaput", but a man with an empty bus who had just finished a 14-hour shift took us all, at no charge, to our rendezvous. Who were all these people? Angels? Finally, a railway crossing had frozen and become impassable, which caused us to have to take a 40-mile diversion each day, but, though we often arrived late, we always got there, for which I praised God, our Supernatural One who never changes.

My worst memory is of us being outside at 9am in a temperature of -27 degrees, dressed in our skirts and tops with black and white Norwegian woollen jackets. We were performing on a platform at the base of the Olympic bobsleigh run. Shivering with cold, and trying to be heard above the roar as each team came in, was a testing time, but I praise God for all that He did – and only He knows what that was. What happens when hundreds of Christians are on the streets, in pubs, prisons, refugee camps, and churches? What happens when there is massive simultaneous intercession? During that time, between 800 and 1,000 Christians were working in three areas. His Word went forth and did not return void, but accomplished what it was sent to do, as promised in Isaiah 55:11.

Tough words

God had a tough message for Norway, which the people did not want to hear. For my speaking on the main stage at Lillehammer, the Lord had given me Matthew 23, which is full of woes for religious people. The soundman sent a message saying, "Jesus would never say that." I sent one back saying, "Read Matthew 23!"

Even some of the King's Kids leaders thought the word was hard, yet, as the children sought the Lord for His programme for a meeting at the police station, one five-year-old boy had Romans 3:23 – "All have sinned." He boldly proclaimed to the assembled policemen, "You are sinners – just like the robbers in your prison." I don't think they enjoyed the challenge. A 17-year-old girl prophesied: "Their hearts are like ice that only the Son can melt." On another occasion, in a church meeting, one of our leaders said, "Repent! Judgment begins in the house of God," based on 1 Peter 4:17. The challenge was made; the response we don't know.

As the Bible says,

> **"Now we see but a poor reflection as in a mirror; then we shall see face to face"** (1 Cor 13:12).

Only God the Father, Son, and Holy Spirit are omniscient.

Chapter 21

Marches for Jesus and Earthquakes in Mexico (1995)

Mexico City is a sprawling capital of around twenty million people with migrants arriving daily in the hope of a job and a brighter future. Spreading over 1,000 square miles, it is also one of the most crowded places on earth. Dicing with death, children sell gum, newspapers, postcards or flowers, to motorists temporarily halted at traffic lights. Poverty and violence has been part of Mexico's life for centuries, yet they are family-orientated, with a built-in gaiety that shines through the gloom.

It is an unhealthy capital, as the encircling mountains trap the polution of factories, cars and endless mini-buses, not forgetting the planes that land and take off regularly, and the debris from volcanic eruptions.

I went to Mexico City with Dr Debra Cole to preach and pray while she held clinic. We worked with dear friends who were leading the YWAM base there. Our first task was to drive eight hours overnight to Zacapu, a town of forty thousand inhabitants. It was early October 1995.

We were invited by four Hispanic-American pastors, originating from this area, to join their programme. First we dedicated a local church, which had been a brothel. This was followed by a big meeting at the Stadium, which resulted in 12 baptisms the next morning in a beautiful river, with cows, horses and washerwomen sharing the same stretch of river. It was hilarious. The event was followed by a 'March for Jesus' ending at the Stadium for another meeting. We participated in the dramas, music, preaching and praying. Many responded to the message.

On Monday, October 9th, there was a 60-second earthquake, 7.6 on the earthquake scale, my first – and I hope last – experience of this phenomenon. As the building swayed, Debbie was taking a shower. I thought I was dying, as I could not stand. Seeing Debbie's dressing gown swaying from side to side on the back of the door made me realise what was happening. Lots of damage was done, but there was not much loss of life. Was God shaking the Zacapu area?

We travelled back to Mexico City via several very poor areas, giving medicines and evangelising in small villages. At one village, like the Macedonians, they gave us much food and a love offering out of their nothing. Sudden rain had ruined their meagre crops.

We were heading for Chiapas, but had to cancel when Hurricane *Roxana* hit that area. Instead we went to a village of brick-makers. The Lord gave me Exodus 1, v14 – revealing their bitterness at their hard task-masters. I preached on this issue, so personal to them. There was a high level of response from old and young, who repented of their bitterness. More salvation followed, as I spoke of the parable of the vineyard where the last to come received the same reward as those who had toiled all day. God is totally just.

Before returning to Mexico City we were invited to lunch with the whole family of our hosts. My friend asked me to preach the Gospel, so I did. It is the same Gospel, yet wealthy people do not seem to respond as do the poor folk. Furthermore, most of them were fully convinced that they were good, despite the Word of God saying that

"all have sinned"
and Jesus said
"None good – except God"
(Luke 18 v19).

Back in the City,.we travelled on the Metro, distributing tracts and engaging in conversations. One appointment, surely Divine, led to three young men praying to receive Jesus as their Saviour right there in the Plaza, with people everywhere.

We worked with many different pastors, but the one I shall never forget is the pastor who asked me to speak in his church, where his four children comprised the worship team. Such a shining face I have not seen before or since, but then he had been taken out and stoned some

87

years earlier for preaching. He had protected his face with his hands, and when he fell, he was left for dead. He wasn't dead but all his fingers were smashed, perhaps never to be healed in this life, on but THAT Day…

Just to add to the excitement, Popocatipetl – the famous Mexican volcano – decided to erupt before we left, covering everything with grey dust.

Truly Mexican know what it is to survive suffering and hardship to sing and dance again. It does hurt to see old people, ascending steps to the Basilica of Guardeloupe on their knees, and dragging baskets of flowers. Jesus only wants a love relationship with us. Isn't He wonderful!

Chapter 22

More Outreaches in Albania
with Dr Debra Cole

For our further visits to Albania, Dr Debbie's medical team and I, armed with medicines, bibles, clothes and on our lips the Word of God, worked with an indigenous church officially registered as Mission Emmanuel in Korce, where the membership was rapidly growing. We went on daily outreach to seventeen different villages, some inaccessible in the winter, to which even the Communists had not managed to get. So their inhabitants had been left in peace, but without almost anything.

They were lovingly treated by Dr Debbie for chronic problems. We had spectacles galore to aid the far and near-sighted. Everybody who asked was prayed for in depth, for healing, deliverance and the breaking of the bonds of wickedness. Five churches were planted. The pastor or teacher was visiting them weekly, and meeting with the believers in all these villages.

The gypsies in Korce had their own church and their own pastor, as a result of Mission Emmanuel also going to them. Fifteen new believers were added to them as a result of our visit, as they had brought their sick to us and saw that Jesus heals!

Most of the villagers said that they were Muslim, Catholic or Orthodox but they readily perceived that they were not, by the word that they heard and as the Way of Salvation was preached.

There were so many exciting stories. Here are a few of them. We asked to visit the home of a 16-year-old boy who had prayed for salvation. As the result of our visit, his 70-year-old grandfather and his grandmother prayed to become followers of Jesus. They had ten children and eighteen grandchildren at that point of time, and I believe that that is the Lord's preferred plan of multiplication of believers. We can read that in Genesis 17, verses 1 and 2.

On one of our visits we went with an American team to Elbarsan and from there went out and visited many very high mountain villages. Later I received a report from one of the American team members and this is what he wrote: "In every village that we visited, we heard testimony from people who had received the Lord during previous visits and how they had trusted God to help and care for their families and how God had been faithful to meet their needs.

"One woman to whom you gave a sweater had unravelled it and then knitted three small sweaters for children." (That's a wonderful thing, because up there in the winter the villagers were so very very cold.)

"In the village of Hochez that you visited with us, a woman came and said that last year, when you were there with us, we prayed for her because she had lost two babies. Six months into a third pregnancy, the doctors had just told her that the baby she was then carrying was dead in her womb. She was, in two days time, to go into the hospital to have the 'dead' baby removed. We prayed – and now that baby is six months old.

I saw it," wrote the American, "with my own eyes.

"In another village a woman came and said that she had had seizures almost every day of her life, but since we prayed, God healed her and she hadn't had single further fit. Another man came and said, "God healed me and I don't walk on crutches any more" – and he jumped up and down to show us how his leg was healed."

These reports were not written by me, but were somebody else's testimony and were a great encouragement to me, because he testified to salvation, to healing, of miracles and deliverance – and that is what the Lord commissioned us to go and do. So visiting Albania has been a very wonderful time for me.

One of the places we went to with the American men was called Blackstones. It was so high in the mountains that I can't tell you how terrifying it was just to drive up there, because the Albanians had no safety barriers for these hair-raising drives over potholes in rusty old vehicles some 3-4,000 feet up. A real test of faith!

In this place called Blackstones, I prayed for many many villagers who came in, mainly lots and lots of Muslim men. I made a salvation call, but I'm afraid that nobody responded. However, you mustn't let that kind of thing get you down, because the Word went forth and *'it will not return void'* as the Bible promises. And this Word did not return void, believe me.

The next day a man came up to me and said, in broken English, "I want you pray my family." He was there with his wife and two children. He said, "I heard you pray someone yesterday and I want that prayer." So we prayed for him, and he went off absolutely delighted. After that, several Muslim men came and said "Will you pray for me?" So we did not go into a barren field. We went into God's harvest field and these men are there in their hundreds all over Albania. So let's pray and pray that God will send and send and send into the harvest there.

Another story I remember is the woman who leapt barefoot over a briar hedge, nothing on her feet – it was so cold up there – so I opened my case, took out a pair of trainers – my size – and gave them to her. She put them on and danced around – dancing, dancing, dancing, filled with joy and laughter. Just because she now had a pair of trainers. How blessed materially most of us are, who live in the West.

I can't say the names of the villages because the Albanian language is very difficult but in a place that I have got written down as Rehova, a woman was dying with cancer. She received Jesus and she went off very happy, and our latest report is that she was still doing well. We saw lots of salvation, lots of healing and lots of deliverance; lots of joy in this precious people who have so little in life and who are grateful for anything.

One of the high places in Albania was totally inaccessible by road so I did try a donkey ride as a means of reaching it. But Albanian women must have muscles that I don't have. They can sit sideways on a donkey on a little piece of wood that is all shiny and slippery, and they manage to maintain their position. But when I tried it, I found myself about to fall off the back of the donkey. I soon gave up that method. Then two men produced a mule and tied me onto its back. They didn't have any saddles or stirrups, and so they tied my feet, with a rope for stirrups, and a small object tied on in front of me, for me to hold on to. It was only as big as my hand.

So I set off to cross a river – happily a shallow river – on this mule and the team walked over a huge long bridge. Suddenly the mule decided that it was thirsty, bent over to have a drink – only God knows how I was protected from falling straight over the front of the mule.

However when I got to the other side, the two men were there waiting, and I said, "Gentlemen, you can untie me, because I'm not going to trust this mule. I'm going to go up on what we British call 'Shank's Pony', which is my own two legs." And that is what the Lord allowed me to do. I managed to walk up – I don't know how many thousand feet – but I had a trick taught me by one of the Albanians of a very easy way to walk, that puts less stress on the lungs or the heart. I was very glad to have heard that piece of information.

I got up there to the high place, right to the top, and I got down again, and to this day I will never understand how I, at the age of 74, was able to do it. A magazine took the story then; ten years later it was not interested. But let me use the story to encourage older readers that you will be surprised what you can do. There's an awful lot that we older people can do in this world.

The final word on Albania. I laugh every time I think of people in the high mountains wearing *Adidas* pants, *Yves St Laurent* T-shirts and *Nike* trainers as they go to milk their goats. What a delightful scene that thought brings to mind.

Chapter 23

Three weeks of Outreach with Dr Debra Cole in Cameroon (1995)

Now to Him who is able to do exceedingly abundantly beyond all that we could ask or think, according to the power that works within us, to Him be the glory in the church and in Christ Jesus, forever and ever. Amen!

Ephesians 3 v20-21

I get excited every time I think of our visit to the West African country of Cameroon. In three weeks there, we did – and saw – amazing things. Our five-man medical team, one administrator and myself were invited in September 1995 by Dr Nick Ngwaryam, a surgeon/urologist, to his Bamenda Clinic. This proved to be in the English-speaking area of Cameroon, in the highlands that border with Nigeria. The north, east and south are French-speaking nations. Cameroon is lovely, very mountainous, with lush foliage. One can see wildlife in the game parks further north, but it is extremely primitive in parts, as we soon discovered.

Tribal warfare had just ended between the Bafanji and Balkumbat people. Burning brands had been tossed into small homes, torching them and their residents. We went to help, however we could. In a village of 14,000, 3,000 were homeless and many injured. The Gospel was preached to the *Fon* (Chief). We emphasised the biblical teaching that *'Vengeance is Mine, says the Lord.'* It caused the *Fon* to think – and he turned from his plan to retaliate in kind. Our team ministered to him, to his many wives (around 50), because he still cared for the old ones, and to his 150-plus children, who were a school in themselves! Sadly, all were sick with various diseases.

This Chief, who had his chair with a silk covering carried behind him, followed us around, observing medical care and hearing more about Jesus. Eventually, he called his whole people together and translated for me himself, because (he said) my translator did not know enough English! There was a huge response. Many were prayed for, some professing immediate healing. The *Fon*, with tears in his eyes, warmly thanked us, asking us to return. We did sleep in his Palace, but it can't have been remarkable, because I can't remember whereabouts in it I slept.

Our next visit was into the jungle via the Presbyterian Hospital at Acha-Tugi, which means 'Waters of Life'. There we ministered to the sick and spent the night. Next day, we headed off by Landrover over horrendous roads to Ajei. Our vehicle tipped onto its side as we traversed huge rocks across the mountainside, down which a river was flowing. We all got the van back onto four wheels, but a little later the axle broke. Our Cameroon driver set off to run many miles back to Acha-Tugi, and returned with a battered lorry. I can see why many Africans can run – and win – marathons.

Arriving at the village at 4pm, we were meet with an incredible sight. The roads were lined with people applauding us. The local *Fon* (Chief), obviously the worse for alchohol, made a lengthy speech of welcome, as did several others – by which time it was too late to hold a clinic, so the medicines we had brought were left for the local nursing staff to use.

The *Fon* insisted that we ate from dishes prepared for us, and that we dance to their music on the village 'green'. He finally presented us with a goat, and this made our journey back to Acha-Tugi even more testing. We donated the goat to the hospital, and were then told that the river we had put our hands in was certainly cholera-infected. We praised God for His protection.

On four separate days we went to the Central Prison of Bamenda. Scabies abounded, as did sexually-transmitted disease, and corruption. The guards were tough; some plainly sadistic, beating prisoners with rubber batons on sensitive areas like elbow joints. Our team treated every sick man, and the Gospel was heard by all as they assembled in the prison yard. Gary and I taught the groups of prisoners that met, claiming to be believers. Most were hungry to learn.

I went to the prison hospital, expecting to pray for the sick, but found that, in this hospital, healthy men, through bribery, had comfortable beds. There I found a proud, tall, handsome man, making raffia hats. His feet were chained, so I knew that he was on a murder charge. I asked him if he were a Christian. He replied that he was. I said, looking him in the eye: "I don't believe that." Some time later, he told all the men, assembled in their denominational groups, this story:

"I went to the latrine (toilet) with my Bible which I was using as toilet paper. I lifted it up to the light to tear off two pages. The light illuminated Isaiah 30. v 15:

"*In repentance and rest you shall be saved.*
In quietness and trust is your strength
but you were not willing."

The Holy Spirit convicted him, so he spent a long time in there repenting. The proud man, John, humbled himself before them all. He also asked me to pray for him. I did, calling on God to save him from the death sentence – to serve Him. These prisoners are in a 'Catch-22' situation. They need money to pay for a lawyer, but unless their family are able and willing to help them, they cannot legitimately get the money.

Some months the former prisoner John sent us this report:

"The old woman – Florence – said that I would be freed – and I was. Before the team came, I was not a fully-committed Christian. But after the preaching and prayers, my life changed. My case was tried. I was found Not Guilty and released."

"Before you came to Bamenda Prison, two prisoners out of every 15 died every month. Out of 674 inmates, 550 were sick and 256 were in a critical condition."

"In the ensuing four months, no prisoners died, and out of the critical cases, 180 said that they were healed miraculously. They all testified in their groups, 92% declaring that they were both physically and spiritually healed. Many gave their lives to Jesus."

"Some have backslidden, because life is hard, but we are praying for them. One man died in my arms, saying: 'I am going home, brother John. Tell the team, I thank them in Jesus' Name.' Those were his last words."

On our final visit to the prison, the Governor decided that we would celebrate, but it had come to our attention that some 150 youths on remand had never been seen. Dr Cole insisted that we would not work or celebrate unless these boys were brought out to receive medical attention and hear the Gospel. Finally the Governor agreed.

These boys were all chained and were so emaciated on their 400 calories a day that some needed huge pins to hold up their shorts: Dr Cole declared that some were near to starvation.

Finally I got to preach. The prisoners called me in 'pidgin' the word for Big Mama. In fact I am small. The Lord gave me Revelation ch 21 v8:

> *"But for the cowardly, unbelieving, abominable murderers, immoral persons, sorcerers, idolaters and all liars, their part will be in the lake that burns with fire and brimstone, which is the second death."*

Great response; some guards walked away. About seventy Moslems turned their backs, but those who received Jesus as their Saviour danced with joy, despite their heavy chains. "To exhort" in pidgin means "to wake up their heart". Many hearts were awakened – and rejoiced.

I had been allowed to go to the women incarcerated there. All had prayer to receive Jesus in their hearts. Two of the nine women were due to be executed for murder. Now they danced out with raffia gifts that they had made for all the members of the team. We then all danced and sang before departing. Glory to God for all that He did!

Add to all that I have told you: the floors and walls that were washed with insecticide purchased by us, as were 600 bars of soap that the men were scrubbed down with by the guards to arrest the scourge of scabies. Add too, the hundreds of strips of plastic purchased for the boys so that they would not have to sleep any more on cold, hard concrete – and the ongoing feeding programme that we set up with the Baptist, Presbyterian, Full Gospel and Catholic women. The time spent with Dr Nick at his clinic, talking and praying. All this in three life-changing weeks. WOW!

Chapter 24

My later active years:
Missions of Reconciliation

In 1995, I found myself in three Missions of Reconciliation, so assumed that the Lord had cut that path for me. Now Reconciliation is a subject that many people don't quite seem to understand. But I'm going to quote a few Scriptures. In Romans 8.26 and Romans 8.34 both Jesus and the Holy Spirit intercede for us, with tears. In Hebrews 5.7, Jesus offered up prayers with loud cries and tears.

In Daniel chapter 9, Daniel confessed his sins and the sins of his people. In Ezra 9.5 to 10.1, both Ezra and the people wept bitterly and prostrated themselves. In Nehemiah chapter 1, Nehemiah confessed the sins of Israel, with repentance, and in 2 Samuel 21, it was not in any way because of David's sin but of Saul's that God had put a famine on the land, and because no-one had done anything about what Saul had done to the Gibeonites with whom Joshua had made a covenant. Saul had broken that covenant, but it was the people of Israel years later, when Saul had long been dead, who were suffering .

In Matthew 23.35, in Jesus' eyes, the Jews of his time were guilty of the blood of both Abel and Zachariah – and the story of Abel goes right back to the beginning of Genesis. In 2 Chronicles 24.21, they stoned to death Zachariah in the Courtyard of the Lord. It would seem that we need to repent of corporate as well as individual sins with tears. Intercessors standing in the gap can identify with present and past sins.

2 Corinthians 5 tells us that we are called to a ministry of reconciliation toward and between men. When we confess to corporate sin about terrible things done by one group of people or a whole nation to another group of people – it does change individuals and nations, and this is one thing I would like to put to you in this chapter.

In 1995 I was invited to go to Glencoe to repent on behalf of the English for what happened at Glencoe. That event was followed by two more, at Culloden and Berwick. This was a learning curve for many of us (it certainly was for me), which, after many more times of confessing and repenting with tears in various countries and situations, those called are working tirelessly with both intercessors and researchers to bring lasting change in nations.

In 1997 I had the privilege of crossing three states in South Africa to ask forgiveness for the 27,000 women and children who died from our neglect in and after the Boer War. We went to nine of the forty 'Koncentration' camps – camps built by the British at the turn of the century long before Hitler. We went to ask forgiveness of the Afrikaans pastors because of what the British done to their people so long before. The pastors were greatly moved as the British team of four prostrated themselves with tears on the prickly, ant-infested or muddy ground. They rushed forward to pick me up and gave me warm hugs. I felt that lots of healing work had taken place.

Then in 1998 I went with others to Australia for nine weeks to confess the sins of our nations both against Australia and the aboriginal people. We needed to acknowledge past sin towards

(1) the convicts

(2) the aboriginals, whom we almost completely wiped out.

(3) The 'stolen generation' where children were forcibly taken from their mothers and given to white families, possibly to breed out the native stock…?? Sadly these children were treated shamefully and often sexually abused.

(4) the 'lost generation' – children in English orphanages were asked, "Who wants to go to Australia?" The children thought that they were being offered a day out, so they raised their hands. Instead they found themselves at sea for what must have seemed years to them. They were treated so badly that I had no trouble in weeping and weeping and weeping every time that I heard these stories. Some of these children weren't even orphans; they were in care because their parents were too poor to look after them.

How had we British sinned against Australia? As we went from Memorial to Memorial of two World Wars, we could see that that country had suffered huge losses – and it is alleged that their forces were put in the most dangerous military positions.

Another thing we did in Australia was to travel a thousand miles into the Outback in search of a man blinded in 1957 by the British testing of an atomic bomb. We found this man, an aboriginal with a very gentle manner, who very graciously received our apologies. I believe that, shortly afterwards, the British Government did accept liability and gave this man compensation.

But the thing which moved me most deeply in Australia was the Fountain of Tears – a sculpture of an eye, with water gently flowing, drop by drop onto the faces of a man, a woman and a child. Despite all that had been done in the past, all the aboriginal leaders who received our apologies did so with the greatest and most gentle humility.

Brian Mills OM, regarded by many as the founder of the prayer movement in the UK, who with Brian Pickering wrote *"Fountains of Tears"* (a Sovereign World International Book, has kindly given permission to include this passage about a two-day Reconciliation Conference in Portsmouth, based on Havant Community Church, attended by intercessory leaders and some Australians.

From page 23 of the Introduction: "Roger Mitchell suggested a time of prayer, discerning that the Lord wanted to lead us. After a while a small, demure lady of seventy-eight, Florence Robertson of Crawley, spoke up. She came out to the front and said: "The Lord is telling me to get one of your Australians on my back." As the delegates watched, totally bemused, the diminutive figure urged the solidly-built Australian, Marilyn, to climb onto her back. She said, "Now, I don't want you to touch the floor or hold on. The Lord's telling me that I have to totally take your body weight." Then Florence started praying, calling on the Lord to forgive our forefathers, to forgive Mother England for abandoning her children, for driving them into poverty and starvation when out of her wealth she should have been caring for them. She asked Marilyn's forgiveness, apologising for the way her great-great-great-great-grandfather had been treated by this so-called God-fearing nation. All of a sudden it was as if the heavens exploded. Everyone in the room was suddenly impacted by the Holy Spirit rushing into the room. It was like a huge spiritual shock wave. It was exhilarating, exciting, awesome, fearsome, refreshing and very, very real.The presence of God, His awesomeness, His hatred of sin, His grace and His healing love were all there in one breathtaking move. For most of the group it was the first experience of prophetic intercessory prayer."

In 1996, I realised that I just 'had' to do as much as I could of the historic Crusaders' Route from Western Europe to Jerusalem. The team started in by going to Clermont Ferrant where in November 1095 Pope Paul Urban II called the Crusades into being. These started from Cologne in 1096. So in 1996 we also started from Cologne and travelled right across Europe to Instanbul.

Then in 1997 I was with a walking team which walked right across Turkey in nine weeks. On to Lebanon and Syria in March 1999, and so finally to Jerusalem in July of that year. That route which we did in stages followed the route of the Crusades nine hundred years earlier, and in the same time-frame of three and a quarter years.

There are many small reconciliations taking place, and there are a few major ones that I know of, planned for the next few years. It is a very very wonderful thing to feel that this humbling of yourself can change a nation. There doesn't seem to be much doubt that Australia has changed because we went. Therefore my heart is to see many, many more people willing to go flat on their faces and weep before the Lord, and ask forgiveness of people who have been so badly treated.

Surely there are many, many of us and many nations who have sinned against other nations, especially on our continent of Europe and I long to see the day – perhaps I will; perhaps I won't – when there will be reconciliation between Africa and the European countries which colonised it – and so Europe can come alive in Christ. That is my heart's desire.

Now it is time to answer the questions that I am most often asked…

Chapter 25

Finance and guidance

"Give, and it will be given to you. A good measure, pressed down, shaken together and running over, will be poured into your lap."

Luke 6:38

"Who finances you, Florence?" "How do you know where to go?" These are questions I have often been asked, and they deserve an answer.

Different provisions

Our creative God has provided for me through many different sources. Some families in my church gave regularly if they knew I was going. Otherwise, it was whoever God spoke to and whatever the Lord told them to give. Here is one example.

On a trip where we were sailing from Ghana to Rotterdam, I had been praying with people all day. At 11pm I went out onto the deck to get some air before retiring. A man was there, and he asked, "Hi, Florence! What have you been doing today – sunbathing?" I told him.

We chatted for a few minutes, and I said "Goodnight" and turned to walk away. He said, "Florence, the Lord has told me to give you a grand." I was speechless, so he added, "That's a thousand dollars!" I replied, "Great, goodnight Paul." Next day, there was a cheque for that amount payable to "Florence": I had to fill in my surname as he didn't know it! That covered my next mission, or even two, and I returned home rejoicing.

A very different avenue of provision has come through one of my two daughters, both of whom are married to Americans. Whenever I visit one of them, her church asks me to share my experiences. As a result of hearing my stories, they have given support to me. This has been a source of provision over several years as they are generous givers. I also received gifts for sharing in churches on all continents.

Open and shut doors

When it comes to effective ministry – knowing where God is directing me to minister – I usually find there are wide-open doors. But, since 1978, I have prayed with two of God's promises in mind. First is His promise in Psalm 32:8-9:

> *"I will instruct you and teach you in the way*
> *you should go; I will counsel you and watch over you.*
> *Do not be like the horse or the mule, which have no*
> *understanding but must be controlled by bit and*
> *bridle or they will not come to you."*

The second is Revelation 3:7 –

> *"What He opens no-one can shut,*
> *and what he shuts no-one can open."*

Then I just take His hand and go with confidence that the door will shut if it is not the Lord's will.

Actually, I only recall one occasion when I got it wrong. I tried to return to Tenerife after a mission with a team from the Anastasis. I wanted to take two people – a mother and her son – from my church who were enthusiastic to "go". It wasn't right, however, so the door shut – on this occasion through the necessary finance not being provided. Naturally, all three of us were disappointed, but we accepted that "disappointments are His Appointments."

I feel confident that if my decisions are not God's will, He will check me. Where He guides, He provides – something I have found to be true time and again.

As for who I join, as far as I am concerned the only thing necessary is that they believe that Jesus Christ, Son of God, died for the sins of all men everywhere and was resurrected, revealed Himself to many, and went to sit at the right hand of God BUT is coming again to rule and reign with His Bride forever. There will be no more marriage, sin, pain, or tears. Hallelujah! Let the Spirit and the Bride say, "Come, Lord Jesus!" Meanwhile, I say: "Go! Go! GO!"

Chapter 26

God's miraculous provision of seats on planes

"Are not all angels ministering spirits sent to serve those who will inherit salvation?"

Heb 1:14 KJV

God has provided for me in many ways over the years. One that I always love is in the provision of seats on aeroplanes. Here are a couple of examples.

In Jamaica

I was homeward bound. I was being escorted by my host, who had invited me to speak at her prayer rooms across Jamaica. In my speaking I had felt led to focus on "Faith". Arriving at the airport for my outbound flight, we discovered that my host could not come into the airport with me. She then wanted to give me her telephone contact number in Kingston "in case I didn't get on"! I replied, "No, that's not faith. I'm believing to go home today."

When a boarding-pass was put in my hand three hours in advance, I felt secure. To my dismay, as the passengers began boarding, I was told by the steward, "No." There was no seat for me! Gradually, the passengers boarded, and I asked three times, "Have you made the head count?" Each time they replied, "Yes." I asked about the jump seats and was assured that they were also taken.

Suddenly I was alone. The steps at the rear of the Jumbo had been taken up. I stepped out on the tarmac and cried, "Lord! Your Word says that 'Faith is the assurance of things hoped for and not yet seen.' I hope to go home on this plane." At that moment, a man dressed in white dungarees ran to the trolley near me and took my case from among three or four others, and raced for the rear of the aircraft.

Simultaneously, a young man ran down the first-class stairs, crying,

"Is anyone waiting? There is one seat available!" I lifted my skirt and ran what seemed like the fastest hundred yards of my life. Arriving in the cabin, I was gasping for breath. and the air hostess said, "You poor dear! You must have been hurrying. Sit down and I'll bring you an orange juice."

My seat was "B", flanked on each side by a passenger. The question is, Whose head was there when they head-counted the passengers three times? Am I implying that an angel had been the extra head until the last possible moment? Yes, I believe so.

Every time I sing the second verse of *Amazing Grace*, "Through many dangers, toils and snares, I have already come," I know that it's true for me and probably for you. Thank God for His protection and provision and for His angels!

In the Dominican Republic

Arriving at Santo Domingo airport in the early morning, I saw that there was chaos. An airline had overbooked by a hundred places, and the crowds were furious, one man even breaking through barriers to chase the plane. Police dragged him back.

I saw a sad-looking duty officer and approached him, saying, "I see you have problems. Just wanted you to know that I'm here." Spotting people who had been on the outreach I had been on, I asked them to pray. Their plane was not due to leave until 11am. They prayed that I might get a flight… "If it be Thy will." I prayed, "God, You know I must get to Puerto Rico to catch the British Airways flight home, and that I don't have money to stay."

Suddenly, I was aware of someone standing beside me. It was the duty officer. He signalled, "Follow me!" We went to a small airline and he spoke to the reservations clerk, then placed me in line and left. In minutes, I was booked on a small plane to Puerto Rico.

Waiting until its departure time of 11.10am, I saw my prayer partners lined up to leave on their flight to Miami. As they reached me the first man shook my hand, saying, "God bless you! We've learned a lesson today." The lady said something similar. Her husband pressed an envelope into my hand addressed to "A WOMAN OF FAITH". In it was US$50, so I went on my way rejoicing!

Arriving in Puerto Rico with three or four hours to spare, I was immediately allocated a seat, as the plane was far from fully booked. I decided to have a bite to eat. The only vacant seat in the food area was with four nuns, so I joined them.

An hour or so later they were inviting me to stay for a few days, which I regretfully had to refuse. However, I left knowing that they had been encouraged and their faith built up, as we talked of what it means to trust God in every situation and for the protection, guidance, and provision He readily gives to those who ask, just as His Word promises in John 14:13-14 –

> *"And I will do whatever you ask in my name, so that the Son may bring glory to the Father. You may ask me for anything in my name, and I will do it."*

Florence's final words to the reader...

Just as Jesus promised in this passage, I have seen Him come through for me time and again during my life. I know that He will do it for you too, if you only ask Him! If the door of opportunity opens before you, then once again I have only three words to say "Go! Go! **Go!**"

Appendix

A List of Florence Robertson's Outreaches

1983	Hong Kong, Malaysia, and Thailand (with FEET Team)
1984	Philippines (second trip)
1985	Switzerland – three school assemblies
1986	Sierra Leone – preaching a two-week crusade
1987	UK – church ministry for three-four weeks in Belfast
1991	Burkino Faso, West Africa – with Dr Debra Cole
1992	USA – speaker at a three-day women's convocation in Texas; also Atlanta, Georgia; and New York with New York City Relief Bus
1992	Albania (second trip) – with US team to the mountain region
1993	Albania (third trip) – with US team to villages
1994	Albania (fourth trip) – more high mountain villages
1995	Albania (fifth trip) – more high mountain villages, and the town of Elbasan
	Macedonia
	Holland – first Reconciliation event at Arnhem
	UK – English/Irish reconciliation event at Ashburnham
	Mexico – YWAM medical clinics in Aacapu and Mexico City
	UK – third English/Scottish Reconciliation event at Glencoe
	France – Crusaders event in Clermond Ferrand
1996	Germany – Cologne
1997	South Africa
	Turkey
	Argentina
1998	UK – Shetlands
	Australia – with Brian Mills
1999	Nicaragua
	Lebanon and Syria
	Czech Republic
	UK
	Morocco
	Israel
2000	Poland
2001	USA – Hawaii
	Mauritania
	UK
	Germany
	Hungary
	Ukraine
	Nicaragua
2002	USA – Hawaii (YWAM writers' school)
2003	Uganda
	UK
	Mozambique
2004	Florence's husband ill; Florence interviewed on *Revelation TV*

Caleb

(Sermon by Andrew Baker, after a prophetic "teaching")

AFTER I HAD ASKED MY PROPHETICALLY-GIFTED FRIEND ANDREW BAKER TO PRAY REGARDING 12 *SPIRIT OF CALEB* TELEVISION PROGRAMMES I WAS ABOUT TO RESEARCH, HOST AND BROADCAST ON **REVELATION TV**, THE LORD WOKE HIM UP ONE NIGHT AND GAVE HIM A TEACHING ON THE SUBJECT – THE SERMON BELOW WAS THE RESULT OF THAT TEACHING

Calebs are people who have dreams and visions, promises and hopes in God and who intend to fulfil them whilst still alive on earth. They are men and women of faith who believe that God will fulfil all He has promised. They don't necessarily need to be 85 but, mature in God, they believe God to enter into the "new thing" that God is doing, and to "take hold" of the part of God's overall plan that concerns them personally.

They are Kingdom-orientated people who faces are set like flint towards His purposes and they won't be swayed or turned right or left, NEITHER will they be moved by what they see.

Giants or opposition simply mean that it's another opportunity for God to show His strength and ability. Their courage will overcome their human fears, because they believe God and march on to that which He has promised. Nevertheless they know God's timing and are willing to wait, even when the weakness or fault or reason for the delay is in others, until God puts things into place for their ultimate victory.

They are Apostolic by nature, pioneers, "TERRITORY TAKERS", going for gold and they carry an anointing to "breakthrough" the enemy lines or holds or fortresses and to take new ground for God.

Their eyes are 'single' and all who oppose will fall by the wayside, and this includes those from within who try to compromise, change or re-direct the vision.

Calebs are men and women of steel-like faith; having been melted, cleaned, shaped and POURED INTO GOD'S MOULD in God's school of life, they are now ready as instruments of war in the Lord's hands. They look not to the strength, size, numbers of the opposition, but the faithfulness and ability of the Lord and Creator of the universe.

Let's look at the story of Caleb in the Bible. In Numbers 13 v6, Caleb is chosen as one of the spies sent to look at the land of Canaan when the Children of Israel were in the desert.

We see in Numbers 13 v17-20 the **instructions** that Moses gave the spies. It was their job to bring back information suitable for a military strategy to be decided on, and knowledge of the agriculture and farming in preparation for the future. Verse 17 –

> *"Then Moses sent them to spy out the land of Canaan and said to them: "Go up this way into the south, and go up to the mountains and see what the land is like, whether the people who dwell into it are strong or good or bad; whether the cities they inhabit are like camps or strongholds; whether the land is rich or poor, and whether there are forests there or not. Be of good courage. And bring back some of the fruit of the land." Now the time was the season of the first ripe grapes."*

Verses 21-25 tell of what the spies did. They spied out the land in many areas and collected huge clusters of grapes to bring back to the camp, along with other fruits of this Promised Land.

Verse 26-29 tell us of the spies' initial report. These are simply facts at this point. Verse 26 -

> *"Now they"* (the spies) *"departed and came back to Moses and Aaron… and brought word to them… and showed them the fruit of the land."*

They said of the land, in verse 27,

Caleb SERMON BY ANDREW BAKER

*"It truly flows with milk and honey and this is its fruit.
Nevertheless the people who dwell in the land are strong, the
cites are fortified and very large; moreover we saw the
descendants of Anak there. The Amalekites dwell in the land
of the south. The Hittites, Jebusites and Amorites dwell in
the mountains, and the Canaanites dwell by the sea and
along the Jordan.*

Next the spies draw their conclusion about the situation and the
possibilities of Israel Making a successful invasion. Let's look first at
what ten of the 12 said (verses 31-33)

*"We are not able to go up against the people for they are
stronger than we are." And they gave the children of Israel
a bad report of the land that they had spied out, saying
"The land is a land that devours its inhabitants and all the
people that we saw in it are men of great stature. There we
saw the giants (the descendants of Anak are from the
giants)… we were like grasshoppers in our own sight,
and so we were in their sight."*

However in verse 30 we read of Caleb's report. In this Joshua, another
of the spies, was to agree with him. ***"Then Caleb quieted the people
before Moses and said, "Let us go up at once and take possession, for
we are well able to overcome it!"*** He comes back with a good report.
He saw everything that the other ten saw, but he and Joshua took **a
different attitude – they chose to believe God**, not what they saw.
The ten saw themselves as nothing, and left out the God factor. Caleb
with Joshua saw themselves as part of God's army and with God on
their side there could be no question of defeat.

When Israel decided IN THE LIGHT OF THESE REPORTS not to go
to the Promised Land, Caleb and Joshua tore their clothes and tried to
reason with the people. Numbers 14 v7 –

*"The land we passed through is an exceedingly good land. If
the Lord delights in us, then He will bring us into this land
and give it to us… only don't rebel against the Lord, NOR
FEAR THE PEOPLE OF THE LAND, FOR THEY ARE OUR
BREAD; **their protection has departed from them,** and
the Lord is with us. Do not fear them."*

So Caleb and Joshua made several points: In verse 30:

(1)   We should go forward into God's plan for us – but in God's timing On this occasion the timing was to be "immediately".

(2)   WE CAN POSSESS SOMETHING WHEN GOD HAS PROMISED IT.

(3)   WE ARE WELL ABLE TO OVERCOME ANYTHING AND ANY ENEMY when God has directed.

(4)   GOD'S PROMISED LAND IS GOOD.

(5)   Caleb alludes to the FACT that God delights in His people.

(6)   GOD THE ALMIGHTY will do the job if we follow Him faithfully and obey His direction.

(7)   Don't FEAR – not anything – people or demons.

(8)   See things through God's eyes – the enemy is just our bread.

(9)   They had spiritual enemies – and realised that the SEASON that God had allowed – whilst the gross, idolatrous sin of these people who lived in Canaan came to maturity – WAS NOW ENDING. It was time for God to pour out His wrath on that which offended Him AND ISRAEL WAS TO PLAY A PART IN THIS OUTPOURING OF GOD'S WRATH.

(10) THE LORD GOD IS WITH US and it was His promise. Caleb and Joshua believed this promise – IT WAS A FACT! Calebs speak this way, but the people of God (Israel) wanted to stone him – and Joshua too. They (according to Hebrews 3) heard but rebelled.

Hebrews 3.19 continues the story and tells us that they could not enter in because of UNBELIEF. Hebrews 4 v2 tells us that they heard the Word but "it did not profit them, NOT BEING MIXED WITH FAITH in those that heard it." In Hebrews 4 v 12 we read the well-known verse about the WORD OF GOD – but We often forget the context in which it was originally spoken:

> *"The Word of God is living, powerful and sharper than any two-edged sword, piercing even to the division of soul and spirit and joints and marrow, and is a discerner of the thoughts and intents of the heart."*

The verse was referring to THE WORD that God had spoken through Abraham and Moses to Israel telling them of the Promised Land ahead of them and how God would Give it to them (Genesis 15 and Exodus 3 v8). The Word, however, DIVIDES MEN from MEN and spotlights the deep motives of the hearts of men. To believe by allowing one's spirit to rule as led by the Holy Spirit OR to REBEL and be in UNBELIEF, allowing one's soul (natural senses) to rule one's decision! This is, and was, the question.

GOD'S DIRECTIVE WORD DIVIDES AND SHOWS what is **in** a man! With the Spies it divided among God's people: 2 for God, 10 against – yes, these were God's people, not heathen. Calebs are led by God's spirit, and have a deep conviction inside that "God is, and that He is a rewarder of those that seek Him." If God has said it, it's a done deal. All they need to do is believe, obey and follow His direction, knowing that HE IS WITH THEM! They have a solid rock-like faith in God Almighty and HIS WORD.

When God speaks a word of promise or direction, we all have a choice of spiritual reaction or soulish reaction. Either can lead us. This was the point that the writer to the Hebrews was making in ch 4 v12. It is a **heart** issue. What was in their hearts? What is in ours? Our heart or spirit need to be decided even before the Word comes. We will believe and follow God, for HE KNOWS BEST.

The Caleb heart is commented on by God in Numbers 14.24:

> *"But my servant Caleb, because he had another spirit*
> *and has followed Me wholly, him will I bring into*
> *the land wherein he went and his seed shall possess it."*

God is pleased with a Caleb spirit.

Returning to our previous point (9) where we commented on Caleb knowing that it was God's season to deal with the sins of those already living in Canaan, we must look back at Genesis and especially at chapter 15. Here God is 'speaking covenant' to Abram. God told him that he (Abram) would not actually own Canaan but that a later generation would return here and attack it and take ownership of it. He told him in Verses 13-15 that Israel would serve another nation for 400 years, but that afterwards they come out with great possessions. Then He told him that in the fourth generation they shall return to the Land, "for the iniquity of the inhabitants will be completed."

Caleb and Joshua knew and believed the scriptures and discerned that it was time to cast out that idol worshippers who did many abominable things before God's face. A Caleb understands things from God's point of view. God was not throwing out a people just to give Israel a land; rather, after years of watching the abominations of these people, He is using the Israelites to wipe out this evil generation from before His face. Calebs know that WHEN IT IS GOD'S TIMING TO DEAL WITH DEMONIC MATTERS, then it is fine to go in and possess something previously used or held by the enemy.

Today we need to realise this too. When the world is becoming more and more liberal in what it accepts as "normal", we are made to feel like those upsetting the peace, when we stand up for God's ways and principles.

Now, for instance, God is fed up with "religion" and is raising a non-religious Church. He is tired of seeing the devil steal, use, abuse and destroy children and young people, and He is raising up a new generation of young believers and many children's rescue workers. He has had His fill of the financial systems of this world, that feed the greed of a few and starve the majority.

Now is God's season for challenging and changing these things, and if we are called to these areas, we can be sure, like Caleb, that God is on the move, and the victory would be assured! The scripture in Numbers 14 v 9 told us of Caleb and Joshua's comments and we are looking at where Caleb says "their protection has departed from them" – referring to the people living in the land of Canaan. Calebs know when God is shielding or protecting someone, or when God is temporarily waiting for a change of attitude and for repentance to come.

Here clearly "time was up" and God's hand was against the people of Canaan, and Caleb knew it. The Amorites and Canaanites only received a reprieve of 40 years because of Israel's sin of unbelief. How many times the action of one person or a nation affects the lives of many others!

Back to our text in Numbers: the people of Israel DID rebel, and God wanted to kill them. Moses interceded on behalf of the people and on behalf of God's good Name. God listened and relented, but said that the people who were in unbelief and rebellion would never go into the land. *"BUT MY SERVANT CALEB, because he has a different spirit in him and he has followed Me fully. I will bring into the land where he went and his descendants shall inherit it."*

This was God's further and personal promise to Caleb.

What a word! Caleb's spirit was in tune with the Holy Spirit. Even though he realized that the people's rebellion meant that he had to WAIT for his inheritance, he was to show great fortitude and patience along with his faith over the coming years until, indeed, God's season came around again. (In Numbers 14 v37-38, God killed the ten by a plague, but Caleb and Joshua lived on; God caused 40 years of wandering in the desert until the entire generation of unbelievers had passed away – STILL CALEB AND JOSHUA LIVED ON.) It was Joshua whom God called eventually to lead the people into Canaan, but God had not forgotten His promise to Caleb. Calebs don't need to be national leaders (although some are). They can even be local – yet supportive of God's national leaders, and their FAITH helps to take the territory.

Let's return to the scriptures for the conclusion of the story. Joshua 14 v-15.

> *"Then the children of Judah came to Joshua at Gilgal, and Caleb said to him, "You know the word which the Lord said to Moses, the man of God, concerning you and mea in Kadesh Barnea!"... He is saying, Joshua! – do you remember what God said to us? Our promise?*

(Reader! DO YOU REMEMBER WHAT GOD SAID TO YOU???).

Caleb continues (v7):

> *"I was 40 years old when Moses... sent me... to spy out the land and I brought back word to him as it was IN MY HEART. Nevertheless my brethren who went up with me made the heart of the people melt, but 'I wholly followed the Lord my God.'"*

> (These are not the word of a prideful man – it's simply who and how He was. A man of simple but rock-like trust in his God.)

(Verse 9) *"So Moses swore that day saying "Surely the land where your foot has trodden shall be your inheritance... And now, behold, THE LORD HAS KEPT ME ALIVE these 45 years"* (Caleb is now 85) *"and yet I am AS STRONG THIS DAY as on the day that Moses sent me. Just as my strength was then, so now is my strength for war. Now therefore GIVE ME THIS MOUNTAIN (with its fortified cities) of which the Lord spoke in that day…It may be that the Lord will be with me"* (humility) *"and I shall be able to drive them out as the Lord said!" And Joshua blessed him and gave Hebron to Caleb as an inheritance… because he wholly followed the Lord God of Israel!"* At this point it was a faith statement. Subsequently Caleb took the mountain (hill country) and it became his inheritance both for himself and his descendants.

Calebs are territory takers and giant killers because they realise that it is "not by might nor by power but by My Spirit, says the Lord." And what of the vision and promises that God has spoken **to you?** *"Let us go up at once and take possession, for we are well able to overcome it."* If God has promised and we follow instructions, it will come to pass! In God's timing, even if the waiting is the fault of others, God will bring it about.

As we stand and believe, like Caleb, to see demonic oppression dealt with and the Kingdom of God established, we will be able to rise up and take territory IN THE SPIRIT that God has promised to us.

Andrew Baker
Makeway Ministries
June, 2004

A Helpful Daily Prayer for those who are called to an 'Impossible' mission but who believe that "with God, all things ARE possible."
Mark 10:27; Num. 10: 34-36

1) And it comes that when I set forward, I will say to the Lord, "Rise up from upon me, O Lord. Go forth and let Your enemied be scattered. And let those who hate You flee before You."

2) And when I rest, I will say to the Lord, "Return O Lord and rest tranquillity upon me for my protection from those that hate You."